Not a Picture Perfect Parent

UNFILTERED MOTHERHOOD FROM BIRTH TO ADULTHOOD

By Betsy Harloff

Published by

1620 SW 5th Avenue
Pompano Beach, Florida 33060
(954)788-4775
editors@editingforauthors.com
dragontreebooks.com

For all the mothers out there struggling in silence, feeling ashamed and alone in a picture-perfect influenced world.

Contents

Note to the Reader

I have created two Spotify playlists as companions to this book.

"Zen Music and Bacon" (Chapter 4): A calm, relaxing playlist to start your morning, practice some yoga, meditate, or wind down in the evening with a cup of herbal tea.

"Not a Picture Perfect Parent": A mix of songs about imperfection, motivation and embracing you, just the way you are.

Enjoy!

Introduction

Have you ever scrolled through your social media accounts, only to feel inadequate thanks to the picture-perfect images you see? Page after page of perfect moments, perfect kids, perfect vacations, and perfect husbands.

Yeah, me too!

In fact, it got so bad I had to leave social media for a while and take a break from all the perfectness of it. I found myself comparing my life to others. I was suffering from a serious case of "the grass is greener on the other side" syndrome. I knew logically that my friends couldn't all have the most amazing, perfect families. After all, we're human, which means we're all flawed and not necessarily living the picture-perfect lives we post on social media.

This is where my book idea came in. What if I wrote a book that was the *opposite* of how perfect my mothering life was? Not a self-help book or guide to be a better mom, but a book built on raw honesty, showing imperfections and mistakes in a time when social media bombards us with picture-perfect images. Little squares of perfection on Instagram, Tweets about perfect lives, and photos added to Facebook albums called "My Blessed Life."

I want you to see and realize that, although most moms look like they have it all together on social media, they are struggling too!

More than ever, there's a great need to show imperfection and normalcy in everyday life. It's not just fashion models and actresses on TV who look perfect; everyday moms are now perfect-looking too!

In a recent article, Nadine Cheung writes that this new "perfect mom" culture on Instagram can be quite dangerous. Moms are posting their "perfectly imperfect" lives, creating the impression that even when life is not so perfect, they still look the part.

There are images of moms suffering from postpartum depression who still look runway ready...or amazing-looking moms in perfectly styled messy buns and stain-free sweatshirts complaining they are such a mess because the baby wouldn't sleep. There are no bags under their eyes and their hair is salon-perfect.

This is doing so much damage, because no one looks perfect when they are in the trenches of motherhood, and very few are brave enough to post those images.

I want this book to sit on your nightstand and be a constant reminder that you are not alone. We are all on the struggle bus. We are all imperfect and trying to figure out this mothering gig, making mistakes along the way.

Parenting is hard—we all make mistakes. There is no manual, and the kicker is that just when you think you've figured it out, life changes and you start all over again. That change could be a new child, a change in jobs, a death in the family, or a serious illness.

We all love to see our fellow moms thrive and grow, but I also know that when we see a mom we look up to make a mistake, it lights up a small flicker in the back of our brains that lets us know we're not alone. She's not perfect either. This makes us feel normal, and with social media throwing perfect pictures at us all hours of the day, it can be hard to remember that we all make mistakes.

This book is not organized in a linear timeframe—it jumps around through twenty years of my life, as I went from zero to five children, sharing how my experiences have changed and morphed yet stayed the same, imperfections, mistakes, flaws and all.

The chapters are set up by topic, with multiple subchapters including different stories or situations. This layout provides a busy mom like you the opportunity to read short sections when you have a few moments between wiping butts and chasing toddlers. Maybe you will be able to knock out a few chapters at a time while you nurse your squirrelly baby who loves to get his foot on your face while nursing. Or maybe you are hiding in the closet eating your stash of chocolate…maybe that's just me!

WHY THIS BOOK?

Over the last year, I have read countless memoirs—and you know which ones I always like best? The ones that showed failures, mistakes, and all the flaws. The raw, uncut versions, showing all the ways they screwed up but kept going and persevered, because you know what? We are all flawed and imperfect, and I believe what we all need to hear is how everyone else is just as flawed as we are. This is especially true in the age of social media, which can bombard us with picture-perfect images. But they are just perfect-looking pictures, not picture-perfect lives. There is a story behind every beautiful photo, and that story is not always as perfect as the picture.

CHAPTER 1

Forgotten

Failure is the opportunity to begin again more intelligently.

—HENRY FORD

Where do I start?

Twenty years is a long time, and that means a lot of mistakes.

I guess I'll start with my worst parenting moment. The term "worst moment" is most certainly subjective—you may find when reading this book that what I thought was my worst moment is not what you'll think was the worst. Still, this is the moment that stands out in my mind.

2004 SOCIOLOGY CLASS

I was twenty-six years old, sitting in a lecture hall at the University of Toledo in my sociology of medicine class. My professor walked in and told us about a story in the news that had recently happened to a colleague at a nearby university. A professor needed to take his child to daycare that morning instead of his wife, who usually dropped their child off. He put his infant into his car and headed off to work. Following his usual routine, he pulled into the drive-thru at his usual coffee shop, ordered a large black coffee with a blueberry muffin, left a dollar tip, and drove on toward the highway.

At work, he parked in the faculty lot, grabbed his coffee, muffin, and brown leather laptop bag from the passenger seat and strode inside, leaving his sleeping child behind. It wasn't until just after lunch that he remembered what he had forgotten in his car. He raced across campus, only to find two students hitting the windows of his blue Impala with tire irons, busting through the glass to reach his infant child. Emergency professionals arrived at the scene at the same time, but it was too late. The child had perished.

My professor asked if we thought a parent should be punished for forgetting a child in the car, literally baking his child to death.

The room fell silent. No one dared to speak, processing this atrocity committed on a helpless infant. His own child!

"He should rot in jail, or better yet, someone should lock him in a car with no way out!" I blurted without thinking.

We all shouted our opinions, but after the shock wore off twenty minutes later, we started coming up with milder punishments. After all, he would have to live with the fact that he had caused his own child's suffering and heinous death. Having to live with this every day seemed punishment enough. I couldn't even imagine how this event changed his life, and thinking about the effect it had on his marriage and family was beyond what I could fully comprehend.

If my husband or anyone else did this to my child, even by accident, I don't know if I could come back from that and forgive them. Even as I sit here and write this, I still feel ill. You know that horrible feeling you get deep in your stomach when you know nothing will ever be the same? That's how I feel every time I recount this story.

While writing this book, I did some research on the story that was presented to us as truth on that day in class. I didn't find any information matching these events, but I did find story after story of parents and caretakers who had experienced this. It even had a name: Forgotten Baby Syndrome. There were also countless articles about parents whose children had almost perished in hot cars.

I may never know for sure if this particular event was real, or if it had been changed to protect his or maybe even her identity. Or maybe it had been fabricated and was just part of this class. But what I do know is that this story stayed with me for sixteen years, and I will never forget the day I heard it.

I judged this parent I didn't know, shaming him and wondering how on earth this could happen to decent, loving parents. I would *never* do something as stupid and careless as that. I mean, really, who does that? Not fully present and loving parents. How could it happen to loving, good parents?

2016 FORGOT ME NOT

Fast forward twelve years. I had tickets to a school presentation of Peter Rabbit at the Valentine Theater, and I was planning to take three of my five children. My oldest, who was sixteen at the time, was taking classes at the university while my youngest child, who was two, was going to stay home with Grandma. She was ten minutes late, so I called her to see what the delay was all about and if everything was okay. It turned out there was some mix-up in our communication and she had just come home from work. She offered to come over anyhow, but I knew she would be exhausted from working all night, so I told her it was no big deal and that I would just take my two-year-old with me.

Now I needed to hurry to get my two-year-old dressed and mentally prepare myself for the two hours of the show that I would not be seeing because I'd be chasing my toddler down the aisles or playing eye spy in the lobby for so long I may want to gouge my own eyes out. I was frazzled getting everyone out the door on time, partly because I really despise being late.

I pulled my van into a parking spot on the side of the road, next to a digital parking meter. I had never used street parking downtown when the kids were with me; I usually just used a parking garage. I grabbed a pile of change to feed the parking meter and told the kids to get out, except for my very quiet toddler in her car seat behind the driver's seat. I left her there because I did not want her wandering away or running toward the street as we fed the parking meter.

The kids happily dropped in coin after coin, watching the digital reader count the money and give us the time we needed to watch the show. In fact, we overfed the meter because everyone was thoroughly enjoying this new urban experience. I didn't mind, as it literally seemed a small price to pay! As our last coins plunked into the meter, friends of ours pulled up into a space four car lengths away.

My three kids were jumping up and down waving as my friend's children ran over. I smiled at my friend Elaine and gave her a small wave, excited about seeing another adult whose company I enjoy. She smiled back, but her hands were too full to wave. She had a travel mug full of peppermint tea in one hand and a blue striped tote with her current read peeking out in the other. I could always count on her for great book suggestions.

I checked to make sure I had my purse and keys, pushed the lock button on the car, and heard that familiar beep signaling that my car was locked.

Elaine was still standing near her SUV, checking to make sure she had all the things she needed while her husband fed the meter.

"Mind if your kids walk in with us?" I asked.

"Sure, go ahead, we'll meet you inside," she shouted over the bustling city noise.

As I reached the theater entrance, I looked back to make sure all the kids who were currently in my care were still with us and not lost in the sea of schoolkids milling around as frantic teachers yelled, "Stay with your buddies and form a single file line!"

I had a strange feeling that something was not quite right. I checked again to make sure I had my keys and my purse, but I still felt like something was missing. I triple-checked—but all the kids were there.

As I walked through the lobby, I remembered thinking that I might be spending some time in the lobby during the show...but why? Why would I be spending time in the lobby and not watching the show?

Then it hit me!

Oh, shit! Bailey!

I was going to be playing I Spy in the lobby with my two-year-old. I started spinning in circles, yelling to the kids around me, "Where is Bailey? Have you seen her?"

They all shrugged. "We haven't seen her," my friend's daughter said.

She was lost...I had lost my baby girl! What was I thinking? Was I not thinking at all?

My stomach felt heavy, my hands trembled, my heart started to race, breathing became difficult, and I was fighting back the bile rising in my throat. My mind quickly cataloged my day, flipping through it like a Rolodex of events that had occurred that morning. What went wrong? Where was my child?

I looked to my oldest daughter, who saw the terror in my dark, wide eyes as I blurted, "I left Bailey in the van, stay here! I need to run back and get her."

I ran back through the lobby, fighting against a sea of schoolchildren spilling through the four sets of double doors. The students were in a tight mass, holding hands and making it difficult for me to pass. I felt like a salmon swimming upstream, but instead of tails and fins hitting me, it was the small hands, heads, and arms of school-aged children eager to be on a field trip. I pushed forward, getting dirty looks along the way.

I couldn't move fast enough.

I reached the theater doors and, like a caged animal being freed, I propelled myself forward with a speed greater than a cheetah. Well, not really...but with adrenaline racing through my bloodstream, it was faster than I would usually run. I was only parked two blocks away. As soon as I rounded the corner, I could see my van parked safely where I left it. I slowed to a light jog, catching my breath. She was safe!

With my eyes locked on my van, I nearly ran over a tall woman wearing bright mustard leggings and a brown floral-print dress. It was my friend Nellie.

"Betsy?" she yelled as I marched past.

"I forgot Bailey in the van," I said, fighting back tears and trying to maintain my composure.

It was a cool fall day, and only fifteen minutes had passed. Bailey wasn't too hot or too cold in the van. She was safe. When I reached the van door, her splotchy tear-streaked face looked at me through the window. My hands were shaking as I fumbled with her car seat buckles. I pulled her to my chest, hugging her tightly and repeating, "I am so sorry...Mommy is here now."

We walked back to the theater, her tiny, precious hand in mine. The walk was slow as I pondered what I had just done and how lucky I was.

When we reached the theater, I found my friends in the box seats that had been reserved for our homeschool group. My three other children were sitting with friends, and everyone was safe. As I collapsed into a seat with my youngest child on my lap, I was reminded of that day in my sociology of medicine class when we heard about the father whose child died because he did something out of routine.

Oh, how I had judged him, thinking there was no way I could ever be that careless...but then I was! The entire show was a blur; I didn't pay any attention to what was going on as "what if" scenarios played on a loop in my head. What if I had left her in there for the full two hours? Would she have been noticed? Would they have broken my window to get her out? Called the police? Stolen her? It was terrifying to think about. How blessed I was to have this turn out okay.

I told the other moms what had happened, not bothering to hide it. How could I? Everyone there had seen me running like a frantic person. I made a mistake, and I felt horrible. No one offered comments or lectured me, there was only silence. Maybe they were silently judging me, but I didn't care. All that mattered was that my child was okay.

NOT JUST ME

Not long after this happened, a friend of mine who was an upper-middle-class, stay-at-home mom posted in a local Facebook parenting group about a similar event that happened to her. She was doing something out of her usual routine and had left her four-year-old son asleep in the back seat. It was a hot summer day, and she was only in the store for twenty minutes before she remembered and went back to the car. By the time she reached the car, the temperature had already gone up quite a bit, but thankfully her son was still asleep and unaware of what had happened. She wrote that she had thought nothing like that could happen to her. Who would forget their kid? She was ashamed and torn with guilt over what could have happened.

Another normal, loving mom who simply forgot. Not because she didn't love her child, but because she had a million things on her mind.

Thankfully, these stories had happy endings, unlike the professor's sad story, but the heartbreaking truth is that every year children die from being left in a car, either intentionally or unintentionally.

The numbers are always highest in July, as it's the hottest month of the year in the U.S. Pediatric vehicular heatstroke (PVH) is no joke, and it happens to the best of parents. Yes, I said best. Since 1998, there have been 794 deaths due to (PVH), and all of these could have been prevented!

In 2018, the average number of children killed by (PVH) rose to over fifty children. Why did this go up? I can only assume that it was caused by our busier lifestyles and the idea that we can do it all.

NEED-BASED CHANGE

This has become such a serious issue that car manufacturers like GMC have added weight sensors to the back seat that chime when you get out, reminding you to check the rear seating. If you don't have a car that does this, I urge you to start leaving your wallet, purse, phone, or any item you need in the back seat with your child. Some websites recommend taking a shoe off and leaving it next to your child. Once your feet hit the concrete, you're sure to remember you are missing a shoe. I am not saying your child is unimportant, but sometimes busy and sleep-deprived parents have a lapse in their memories, especially when things happen out of routine.

For me, this was one of my worst moments as a parent. My daughter was safe, and it turned out okay, but I have never stopped thinking about what could have happened. This was not the first time I have lost or forgotten a child, and it was not the last either. I'll talk more about those instances in a later chapter.

Mamas, I am here to tell you that you cannot do it all. Ask for help, and stop trying to be as perfect as your friends seem in their social media posts. They are struggling too! Our brains are not wired to multitask. Can we multitask? Yes, but at what cost? When you are dividing your time and energy between a million tasks, things will inevitably fall through the cracks. Forgetting something important doesn't discriminate by race, class, or gender. It could happen to anyone.

Mamas,
I AM HERE TO TELL
YOU THAT YOU
CANNOT DO IT ALL.
Ask for help, and
stop trying to be
as perfect
AS YOUR FRIENDS
SEEM IN THEIR
SOCIAL MEDIA
POSTS.

CHAPTER 2

Ten Little Fingers and Ten Little Toes

In October of 2000, I gave birth to my first child, which kick-started my never-ending journey into motherhood. My miracle baby, the child doctors said my husband and I couldn't possibly conceive. He was meant to be, no matter what the doctors said—life was created without intervention and without us knowing. He was a complete surprise, and I was overjoyed to be the mom I always knew was in me.

No, I was not one of those women who went to the hospital thinking they had the flu only to find out they were pregnant. His conception was a surprise. I was even on the Depo-Provera shot... talk about a miracle!

I sometimes refer to him as my rough draft, the child who taught me so much about parenting. Even after five kids, I am still learning. But I believe I made the most mistakes with my first child, my miracle baby.

THE MISSING TOE

So here is this beautiful little boy, with ten perfect fingers and ten perfect toes.

Well, they were perfect...until I cut off his toe!

Okay, don't panic. It wasn't his whole toe, just the tip!

Sebastian was just a few weeks old when I realized I needed to take on the scary task of trimming his ferociously sharp nails. How did they even get this sharp? He hated those mittens, and besides, how hard could it really be to cut a tiny person's nails? I'd been cutting my own for more than two decades.

What I didn't know was that infant fingernails are very thin; how they can be so thin yet so sharp is truly a wonder to me. It took well over an hour to trim his fingers, and I couldn't do it while he was awake because the moment I grabbed his little hand, he would pull away and flail angrily. So, I needed to wait until he was asleep to quickly get one nail done at a time, all while I was holding him and rocking.

I held my sleeping baby while I trimmed his fingernails, but when I got to his toes, things became more difficult. How could I hold my baby and trim his toenails at the same time? I couldn't, unless I laid him down. The first foot went smoothly, and after finishing fifteen infant nails flawlessly (including his hands), I got a little cocky. I grabbed my son's foot and lined up the nail clippers with his sixteenth nail—the big one on his right foot. Just as I pushed the metal clippers together, he tried to pull away. My alignment was off, and I squeezed down, taking off more than just his nail. A blood-curdling scream filled the room. Joe, my husband, jumped up and ran over.

"What happened? Is he okay?" he asked with great concern, looking over my shoulder at our infant son.

"I...I...I...was just trimming his nail and he moved. I took off too much!" I shrieked, tears running down my face. "Go get a cold, wet washcloth."

Joe rushed to the bathroom while I scooped up my profusely bleeding baby. I rocked him, held him tight, and kept saying in a sobbing and shaky voice, "I am so sorry." Joe handed me the wash-cloth, which Sebastian mostly bled through before Joe went to get a new one. I held the washcloth to his toe for a very long time to stop the bleeding, soothing him and rocking him to sleep. When he was calm and asleep, I carefully removed the washcloth and inspected his toe more closely. I had cut off most of his nail and the tip of his toe. What an idiot I was. You see, that's what happens when you get overly cocky and extra confident in life—the universe has a way of shutting that down. I applied an antibiotic cream and a large bandage, then carefully put on his blue and white sleeper.

A few weeks later, I was folding laundry on the futon in the living room of our small apartment while Sebastian slept next to me. Just as I grabbed the sleeper Sebastian was wearing during "the night of the missing toe," Joe walked past. "What the hell is that?" he said. "Did you cut him again?"

"No," I said, irritated by his interrogation. "This was the sleeper he was wearing the night I trimmed his toenail too close. His Band-Aid came off when he was sleeping, soaking his sleeper and part of his crib sheet!"

"Wow! That's a lot of blood!"

"I know, I was so surprised when I got him that morning. This is my favorite sleeper of his, but I couldn't get the stain out. I'm not sure I want to keep it now…every time I look at it, I'm so heart-broken and disappointed in myself."

"You should save it so he can look back as an adult on the day his mom took off his toe!" He chuckled.

"Stop it! That's not nice, don't be a dick! I'm throwing it away. I don't want any proof that I did this. It makes me too sad." I immediately got up and threw the sleeper in the trash, fighting back the tears. I already felt bad enough, Joe's mocking only made it that much worse.

Joe was very sarcastic and very serious when he used sarcasm. It was hard to tell when he was being serious and when he wasn't. At this early point in our relationship, I wasn't good at discerning whether he was being sarcastic or serious. A later conversation revealed that he was being sarcastic and didn't realize that I took him seriously. He genuinely believes I would never hurt our children and that I always have their best interest at heart. Before I understood his tone and use of sarcasm, I shed many tears privately, some days literally in the closet.

Sebastian's toe healed just fine, and you can't tell there was ever an incident. Later, when I was in my thirties, I was using a mandoline slicer to cut potatoes for a knock-off recipe of Olive Garden's delicious Zuppa Toscana soup. I didn't use the safety guard, again because I was feeling confident and cocky and had done it many times before. Of course I sheared off the tip of my finger like a slice of potato. I didn't think it would ever heal correctly. I thought maybe I would have a lopsided finger forever. But it healed just fine, like Sebastian's toe. Still, every time I look at my finger, I'm brought back to that day I took off part of my baby's toe...

HE SHOULD'VE WORN A HELMET

It's a wonder that my oldest managed to make it through infancy. When he was little, I had an old two-door aqua Dodge Shadow, and my son's infant car seat was a used one I purchased from a friend who'd just had twins. I didn't have a lot of money, so I bought what I could afford used.

I installed the car seat in the center of the back seat, then I had it inspected to make sure I did it properly and that my precious cargo was safe. However, it was troublesome to wrangle the infant carrier in and out of the back seat. Most times, I just left the car seat in the car, lifting him out of the seat and carrying him. He hated the seat anyhow and always wanted to be held, so using the seat was just a bulky pain in the ass.

This wasn't the best solution either. It was challenging to climb halfway into the back seat with the front seat folded down, and I often hit his poor little head on the top of the door either getting in or out. You'd think I would learn the first time and never do it again, but I did this over and over. Using Joe's car was not an

I am not perfect.
I NEVER PRETEND TO BE
PERFECT. BUT I OWN UP TO
MY FAILURES,
*because my failures
made me a better
mother and person.*
I KNOW PEOPLE SAY THIS
ALL THE TIME, BUT IT'S
THE HARDCORE TRUTH.
*without mistakes we
would never learn to
be better people.*

option, either, as he had a Dodge Neon, which was even smaller. Things didn't change until one day I hit his head so hard he got a welt. The mom guilt is still strong on this one. How could I have been so careless?

I am not perfect. I never pretend to be perfect. But I own up to my failures, because my failures made me a better mother and person. I know people say this all the time, but it's the hardcore truth. Without mistakes we would never learn to be better people.

I do feel bad for my firstborn because I made the most mistakes with him, but he still turned out to be a wicked smart adult. He started college at fourteen, graduating magna cum laude at nineteen with his bachelor's degree in media communication. I did a lot of things wrong—loads of my mistakes are included in this book—but I did a few things right too.

Over time, I did eventually stop hitting my poor child's head on the door frame of the car, but maybe he just learned to duck!

HUMPTY DUMPTY HAD A GREAT FALL

When Sebastian was around six months old we took him to get his pictures taken at JCPenney's. This was just before everyone owned a DSLR. The studio was a traditional photo studio; Sebastian was dressed in denim overalls with no shirt, knockoff tan Timberland boots, and a navy do-rag tied around his head. He looked like a miniature construction worker or tough man. The photographer loved his look and had many props to complete it. We put Sebastian on a short table, about three feet high, with a black tablecloth and dark wooden beams in front of him. Sebastian had just learned to sit up unassisted, but he sometimes fell over, so I kept my hand near his back just in case.

"Your hand is in the picture," the photographer said. "Can you move a few feet away so I can snap a really great photo of him? I will be super-fast...this is going to be a great picture."

I'm not sure why I listened to her—maybe I really wanted that super-cute picture for my wall. I was young and naïve, so I listened without question. She made my son laugh hard, capturing a cute photo a split second before he lost his balance and fell backward off the table and onto the concrete floor. An ear-piercing scream echoed throughout the studio. I quickly scooped up my baby, who had a dark blue goose egg growing on his head before our eyes like some weird magic. It was terrifying. Everyone crowded around. I was feeling claustrophobic, so I pushed past and walked to the corridor just outside the studio to calm and soothe my baby.

People left me alone—they gave me the distance I needed to calm my child. His crying subsided, leaving him huffing and gasping. I carried my puffy-eyed, red-cheeked baby back into the studio. They handed me an ice pack, along with countless apologies and a voucher for an entire year of free photoshoots.

To this day, I think those photos are my favorites. They are truly some of most adorable pictures. They don't hang on my walls—they stay packed away. Looking at them brings me back to that horrible mistake.

Over the last twenty years, whenever Sebastian did something brainless or stupid, we would joke that we should've sued JCPenney's, insinuating that his fall had caused him brain damage because that could be the only reason that a truly smart child could do some really idiotic things. Over time, Sebastian started to get a complex about it, thinking that he really was brain damaged, so we stopped teasing him about it.

How could I have been so naïve to listen to that photographer? Clearly, it all turned out okay, but what if it hadn't? Why didn't I just trust my gut? I should've never left his side. I'm still troubled that he fell because of my stupidity, but I never made that mistake again.

THIS TASTES SHIT—A CRAPPY PARENTING MOMENT

It was mid-morning, with the sun streaming through the window of our two-bedroom apartment, creating a lovely magical glow in the room. I had just finished changing Sebastian on the worn brown carpet in his bedroom. He was now ten months old and fully mobile. He could crawl like a pro and even take a few steps when he chose to.

I hoisted him up to a sitting position and left the room to throw away the poopy diaper. When I came back in, I found Sebastian next to his basket full of stuffed toys. He was joyfully taking them out one by one, then putting them back in, over and over. It was the "dump and fill" milestone. He loved this game and played it all the time, which is why we had so many baskets full of different types and textures of toys. I would sit with him and call out the names of each item he pulled out, then repeat the name as he replaced it in the basket.

After fifteen minutes or so, he got bored with his game and crawled away. He reached for something near his crib and put it in his mouth; I figured it was a crumb that had fallen from his crib. Back then, I kept an immaculate house. I vacuumed every day, everything had a place, and it was generally spotless. (Fast forward to present day with five kids: my house is a mess! Back then, though, my friends used to call me Monica from the hit TV show *Friends* because I suffered from OCD and neurotically cleaned all day.)

I had just vacuumed his room that morning, so there was nothing on the floor. Or so I thought. After he put the crumb in his mouth, he made a weird face and pushed his tongue out. Then he grabbed something from his mouth with his chubby little hands, looked at it, and put it back in his mouth.

I moved closer to figure out what on earth he had. I stuck my finger in his mouth and did a finger sweep, removing a hard, toffee-colored ball from his mouth. It looked like a small grape, but it was dark brown, hard, and slimy. I lifted it to my nose so I could smell it, then threw it down when I realized what it was.

SHIT!

My baby was eating SHIT while I watched him make weird faces! I ran to the bathroom to get a wet washcloth to scrub off his tongue and mouth, then I rinsed and scrubbed his mouth over and over again.

My son is going to get sick from E. coli. Maybe I will get E. coli too!

I pulled out some Lysol disinfectant wipes and used them on the carpet, his hands, my hands, and all surfaces nearby. I'm sure it was overkill, but I was a bit of a germ freak back then.

I couldn't figure out how a small, marble-like turd ended up on his floor. Then I remembered: when I had changed Sebastian an hour earlier he was constipated, so there were five or six small round and very hard poops in his diaper. When I rolled up the diaper to throw it away, one must have rolled out.

With all the mistakes I have made with Sebastian, he still gets a lot of backlash from us because we are smartass parents who bring up these things often. Any time something tastes bad or off, we joke that Sebastian should taste it because he's the only one who truly knows what shit tastes like.

SHAKEN BABY SYNDROME

Before I had children, I never understood how a parent or caregiver could get so frustrated by a crying child that they would shake the baby hard enough to cause brain damage. Oh, how we judge others when we have not walked in their shoes! I hadn't been around an infant for long enough yet that the sound of a crying baby bothered me—until the day it did.

Sebastian was born with all sorts of stomach issues. After my inability to breastfeed, which was really just ignorance and poor information, I switched him from formula to formula. No matter what brand or type I chose, my poor baby had horrible diarrhea and vomiting—not spit-up, but projectile vomiting an entire bottle just after he ate and drenching both of us. It was a miracle that he was such a fat, healthy baby. The doctors never wanted to look further into his stomach issues because he was gaining weight and thriving. They just classified him as a colicky baby. Colic is just a generic term for a baby who cries suddenly for hours and hours and can't be consoled. Besides crying, symptoms include a hard stomach, gas, pulling the legs up to the chest as a sign of constipation, and frequent spitting up. There is no diagnostic test; it's just a catch-all diagnosis.

Sebastian cried all the time. He would sometimes shriek for hours. I would walk, bounce, rock, and sway with him in my arms, but only time would cease his crying. It was so hard for me as a new mom to feel confident in my parenting skills when I could not soothe my own baby. What kind of mom was I? This caused me to fall into a deep depression. I felt like a failure, and I didn't want anyone to know, fearing they would see me as the incompetent mother I felt like I was.

Joe worked full time as a computer tech at a local electronic store. When he got off work, most days he went to a game room to play with his friends. He never wanted children; he had a horrible father and feared he would end up treating his own children as bad as he was treated. He wanted to break the cycle, so he did only what was necessary with us, the absolute bare minimum.

When he was home, he was not *really* there. He fed Sebastian with a bottle propped up on something, not even holding him and completely disconnected to the little life he had helped create. Later, I discovered that he was afraid he would break him, so he had propped Sebastian up. He would take on parenting tasks, but only if I asked. He never volunteered. So I only asked when I felt like I was going to lose my mind. How do you ask someone to help you care for a baby they didn't want?

When I was in labor, he stayed on the opposite side of the room, never coming near me. I understand it must have been difficult for him to be put into the role of a father when he never wanted to be one, but I'd rather not have him there at all if he was just going to ignore me. I should have left him, but I was scared and weak. I told him that I could raise this baby on my own, but he refused to sign away rights.

As soon as Sebastian was born, Joe left the hospital and didn't come back for thirty-six hours. When he finally made his appearance, he was carrying a stuffed alligator pillow and fell asleep on the hospital bed while I sat in the chair holding my miracle baby and waiting to get released. I am forever thankful that I was able to be a stay-at-home mom during this crucial stage of development, but I was doing it on my own. The only difference was that I didn't have to work, because Joe provided the income. I was essentially a solo parent! After weeks of being home alone with my screaming baby and suffering from postpartum depression, I lost it.

I hadn't seen Joe for more than five minutes in days. He came home every night just after 1 a.m., after I had fallen asleep from the 12 a.m. feeding. He took on the 3 a.m. feeding, which provided me with just under six hours of uninterrupted sleep a night, which was amazing!

It was about seven in the evening, and Sebastian had been crying for hours. I finally called Joe, lost in frustration.

"Hey, Sebastian won't stop crying. I just don't know what to do."

"Put him in his crib, shut the door, and walk away. You hold him too much. He'll cry himself to sleep."

I should've expected this answer.

I didn't have anyone else to call. I was twenty-three years old, and none of my close friends had children yet, so they would be no help. Leaving my crying baby alone in a room was just not an option. So I rocked more—until I lost it. I grabbed my baby with a quick, jerking motion and screamed loudly in his face: "Why won't you stop crying? I'm doing the best that I can!"

His cry quickly changed to a higher-pitched squeal of terror as the person he loved and trusted most terrified him. I immediately pulled him to my chest, whispering over and over in his ear, "I am so sorry, I am so sorry, I am so sorry. Mommy is here. I will never again do that to you!" And I never did.

As soon as I wrote these words, I walked over to my now-nineteen-year-old son and told him what I did with tears in my eyes and apologized.

"Well, I don't even remember that!" he said.

"Well, you wouldn't, on account of the brain damage that you suffered that day. Just kidding. You don't have brain damage. Well, maybe a little from the fall at JCPenney's," I said, giggling.

"Mooooom, STOP!"

"Okay, okay, you know you're my smart and mostly perfect child, and I'm so sorry that you were my first draft and the one I may have made the most mistakes with. You have been, and always will be, my first child. The child who opened my heart and soul, the child who made me realize that I will never love anyone more than my children. I'm your Mama Bear, and I will viciously attack anyone who hurts you, so I'm sorry that I was the one who sometimes hurt you. I wish I could take it back."

"Okay, Mom, you're being weird. Can you go back in the other room and continue writing?"

I smiled and walked away, knowing that despite my failures, he turned out to be a fantastic kid.

PUT ICE CUBES ON HIS FEET

I'm not sure if I read this in a crappy parenting book, blog, or online article. Maybe I came up with this gem on my own. As a baby, Sebastian always wanted to doze off around 7–8 p.m. after his last feeding. We wanted him to sleep through the night, so we started putting cold washcloths and ice cubes on his feet to prevent him from falling asleep before his midnight feeding, when he would doze off after he finished his bottle. We thought we were parenting geniuses.

After the ice-cube treatment, he would only wake up 50 percent of the time for another feeding at three in the morning, which Joe took care of. If people knew we were putting ice cubes on our baby's feet, child protective services may have been called. I cannot believe I was okay with this, and that it may have even been my idea. I was too sleep deprived to remember.

Weeks later, I read that overtired children have a harder time sleeping and that an earlier bedtime can be the solution to help children sleep longer. What? That was crazy: how can an overtired child not be able to fall asleep and stay asleep? If I am overtired, I pass out the moment my head hits the pillow or any other soft surface…or sometimes even a hard surface.

We decided an early bedtime was worth a try—we had nothing to lose. I fed Sebastian his early evening bottle at 7 p.m., but instead of keeping him awake until midnight with ice cubes on his feet I let him drift off into a sweet cuddly slumber in my arms. I waited until he was in a deep sleep before I placed him gently in his bed. Can you guess what happened? He slept. For twelve hours, all the way through to 7 a.m. We kept checking on him to make sure he was breathing—and he was! He tossed and turned a few times, but he never cried and never woke up.

I didn't sleep well that night; it was strange and highly unusual for him to sleep that long. We scratched our heads in bewilderment and tried again the next night, thinking it wouldn't work twice in a row. But guess what? He slept through twelve hours again! We tried this for many nights with the same result: he kept on sleeping through the night.

To this day, my mind is still boggled over how an overtired child can have a harder time falling asleep and staying asleep. I'm sure there is some science to back this up, but I never cared to spend my free time figuring out how this works. I was just so happy to know that it worked!

I often look back on all those lost hours when I should've been putting my child to bed sooner, and I know that at least I figured this out with my first child. We had four more children after Sebastian, and we went forward into our parenting adventure knowing that overtired children don't sleep.

TURN ON THE VACUUM AND WALK AWAY

We can all agree that the sound of an infant crying is very unpleasant...but why? Researchers using magnetoencephalography, which is a noninvasive technique that detects and records the magnetic field associated with electrical activity in the brain, found that even if you are not a parent, the sound of an infant crying lights up areas of our brain responsible for the "fight or flight" response. This response is in our DNA…it's an involuntary action that makes us want to help the crying baby.

Not so shocking are the many cases of abuse and Shaken Baby Syndrome that have happened when people are exposed to prolonged crying from a baby. This is why a support system is needed for new mothers—I was so close to my own breaking point the day I grabbed my son and screamed into his face. No one could've loved my baby more than me, but there I was committing an abhorrent act upon my child.

At the time, I was alone, a solo mom trying to raise a baby with an absent father. I sometimes think back to that time and wonder if it would've been better if I had raised our son alone and moved out. But then I would have had to share custody, and thoughts of Joe leaving Sebastian to cry alone in his crib broke me. I knew without a doubt that I needed to stay for my boy. I wanted him to have a loving father in his life. I wanted to give our family a chance. I hoped that, over time, things would change for the better. I also worried about my own sanity: what if I snapped again? What if it was worse? Joe might not have been around much, but he was around sometimes.

Knowing that staying was my only option, I knew I needed to find some ways to cope. I found a mom tribe online. These were moms going through similar situations. I also researched coping mechanisms for dealing with the stress of a crying baby. The three things I did when I knew I was close to a breaking point were:

1. Place Sebastian in a bouncy seat in his room. This was crucial because he had reflux and vomited often, so keeping him inclined was the key to minimizing any chances of aspiration. I would also position him so that if I cracked the door to check on him, I could see him but he couldn't see me. I would strap him in nice and tight, partly close the door, and walk out of the room. He was not happy with this—he would scream and wail loudly. In response, I would flip on

the vacuum, making sure I turned off the rotating bar so I would not burn a belt up and let it drown out the sound of his crying. Usually I would sit in the hallway and cry, but I knew this was a better alternative than snapping and unintentionally harming my baby. Maybe the hysterical crying was even good for us, as a hard cry releases endorphins. I would only let this go on for between five to twenty minutes. Sometimes he'd fall asleep...other times he would still be crying, but he usually nodded off not too long after I picked him back up.

2. Working out. This is a fantastic way to release stress because it also releases endorphins. We didn't have cable TV or much money to spend on workout videos, but fortunately PBS played a series of fitness videos, beginning at six in the morning. Sebastian was usually awake by 7 a.m., so after I fed him a bottle, I would place him in his bouncy seat in front of me and do a free thirty-minute workout. This usually consisted of Yoga by Yoga Zone or Bodies in Motion by Gilad Janklowicz, depending on when I was done feeding him. This was 2001, so I could record these videos on my VCR to play them later. This provided me with the opportunity to watch it later in the day and work out during nap time.

3. Knowing it was okay to set my baby down. This may seem like a no-brainer, but I felt like a failure every time he cried, like I was doing something wrong and was a bad mother. When it came to setting him down, the cradle swing was my saving grace. Front-to-back swings only accentuated his reflux, but the side-to-side swing was a game-changer. At first he didn't like it—I think he was really just protesting being put down. It took just over a week of crying for him to realize that it was quite nice. After much

trial and error, I discovered the sweet spot of mid-afternoons. If I placed him in his swing after lunch, he would peacefully drift off to sleep without crying and stay there for up to ninety minutes. This new routine gave me time to take a long, hot shower. I'd let the hot water flow over me like silky vanilla and lavender-scented ribbons, washing away all my stress. I also had the time to shave my legs to a nice smooth finish, unlike the Sasquatch look I had going on. Never underestimate the power of a long, hot, uninterrupted shower. I also started cooking real meals, unlike the random food I had been stuffing in my mouth all day in between feedings and diaper changes. Some days I'd sit at my desk and check in with my online mama tribe. These women, strangers to me at first and spread across the US, helped me through this rough patch, and I started to feel like a person again.

I once judged Joe for wanting to leave our child to cry when nothing else worked, and then I ended up doing the same. Joe had a hard transition to make from a young boy who was deeply hurt by his own father to accepting his own role as a good dad. When he chose to stay, he had already made that first step without knowing he was doing so.

Parenting is hard, especially during that first year. It can test the limits of the strongest relationships. We did the best we could at the time, and through writing this book, so many conversations were brought to light, allowing healing to begin. I had no idea until this year that he propped the bottle up to feed Sebastian because he was afraid he would break his son if he held him. All I saw was neglect.

I urge you to have the difficult conversations so you can move past emotional pain and trauma. It took me twenty years and writing this book to initiate some of those conversations.

WILL THEY JUDGE ME IF I JUST READ A BOOK IN THE LOCKER ROOM AND NOT WORKOUT?

Things got better. I lost a lot of weight, and I learned to cope. I started feeling like me again. Just before Sebastian's first birthday, I joined an all-female gym, which was not as important as the fact that it had childcare and was extremely affordable at only fourteen dollars a month. The gym was open six days a week, and I made use of each day. I had gained a whopping eighty pounds with my son—and that was *after* I birthed his 9 lb., 11 oz. butt! I was already down thirty pounds from my free PBS station workouts, but I still had fifty more to go.

At first, Sebastian hated the daycare at the gym, crying the entire time. It was a small windowless room, about the size of a large living room, full of toys and usually three or four daycare workers. They were all great at helping him adjust and reassuring me he would be okay. At first, he was hysterical, but they ushered me out of the room quickly.

"It really is easier for everyone if you get out fast. Trust me, he will stop crying. If he doesn't, I promise I'll come and get you," the daycare worker said as I stared into her brilliant, light-blue eyes surrounded by deep laugh wrinkles. She had a comforting look about her; I felt she could be trusted. Maybe someday when my kids are all grown and I'm a grandmother, I'll pick up a part-time job at a gym daycare to comfort other young mothers.

So I gave Sebastian a quick kiss and reluctantly left the room, shutting the door behind me and heading to the elliptical machine. Twenty minutes later, she walked over, letting me know that he was no longer crying and happily playing. Whew! My heart would always sink as she approached—I thought she was coming to get me because he wouldn't stop crying. She assured me that if a child cried for too long they would come and get the mother anyhow.

This went on for three weeks. After that, he would only cry for a few minutes, then go on happily playing with the Matchbox cars

27

from a yellow bin on the bottom shelf. They were his favorite. The days ticked by and the weight melted off. Before I knew it, I had dropped all fifty pounds, bringing me back to the small hourglass shape I once had.

Of course, there were days I didn't feel like working out, but I went anyway. On these days I would lazily ride the stationary bike, reading romance novels by Nora Roberts or a science mystery by Robin Cook. This hour a day at the gym was literally the only alone time I had. Joe was still nonexistent. When he did grace me with his presence, it was only to eat whatever I had cooked for dinner before planting his butt at his computer chair to play massive multiplayer online role-playing games and completely ignore us.

When Sebastian was about seven months old, I started sitting him on Joe's shoulder like a parrot, while Joe was at the computer. This was the only attention we got, and it was forced. Recently we came across a photo of this, and Joe commented that he loved it and thought it was so cute. I looked at this picture and was reminded about how starved for attention Sebastian and I were.

Today, Joe sees this situation in a totally different way—he thought he *was* spending time with Sebastian. Clearly, we had contrasting ideas of what spending time meant. Over time, Joe slowly started opening up to the possibility of being a father in more than just name. He started spending more time away from his computer and enjoyed outings to our local parks, where we would watch Sebastian run the trails ahead of us with so much energy.

The gym was my main outlet for stress reduction. There were days I didn't want to get on the elliptical or do a fitness class, so those days I'd do what I called "the lazy mom workout." I'd get on the reclined stationary bike for sixty minutes and read a book— usually a romance novel, because that was the only romance in my life at the time.

Some days I just wanted to sit in the locker room and read. I often wondered what the gym employees would say if I just dropped my child off in the daycare room, then sprawled across the wooden locker room benches to read a book. Turns out this one hour a day was the catalyst I desperately needed to get me back to my pre-mom body and start feeling like me again…not just physically, but mentally too!

A lot of mistakes were made as a new mom, and as I continued on to have four more children, more mistakes were made. I learned from those mistakes and never made the same one twice.

CHAPTER 3

Crunchy Mamas

Some of you may not know what the term "crunchy mom" means. I didn't until I was called one and had to ask the meaning. A crunchy mom is one who supports some of the following:

Attachment parenting
Co-sleeping
Baby wearing
Cloth diapering
Practicing elimination communication
Natural birth, water birth, or home birth
Delayed cord clamping
Breastfeeding, sometimes continuing long after the baby is
    two years old
Using ecofriendly products
Not supportive of circumcision
Using a delayed vaccine schedule or selectively vaccinating
Using holistic medicine and alternative health methods
Homeschooling, unschooling, or Montessori schooling
Kombucha drinking, vegan, organic food only
Owns chickens or goats and allows them to free-range
Love of natural products

Very hippy dippy with a respect and love of nature
Chemical-free cleaning, using only vinegar and essential oils
Toxin aware
A social activist that leans to the left
A fond love of Mason jars and hand-knitted items
Practices family cloth
And so many more…

This is not an inclusive list by far, but if you support some of these, you may be a crunchy mom too!

THE AGE OF ORGANICS

Organic food is not a new concept: it's been talked about since 1924 when Rudolf Steiner spoke out about going back to the natural ways of farming without machines or chemicals. Crazy to imagine that way back then, organic food was being talked about. People quickly realized after the Industrial Revolution that factory farming feeds many, but at the great cost of losing nutrients in foods. It wasn't until recently that new USDA standards were established for organic food so consumers could find items with the USDA organic label on the shelves of their favorite stores.

ORGANIC BREASTMILK

Although you may not get a certified USDA stamp across your breasts, if you eat a clean diet of mostly organic foods, your breastmilk could be considered organic.

I was determined to make breastfeeding work with my second child. I was unsuccessful with my first—he just couldn't latch properly. I would pump, but even bottle nipples were hard for him. I tried every single bottle nipple until I found an orthodontic nipple made by Playtex. It was a weird flat nipple, but my baby could eat, and I felt like I had failed. I couldn't perform the most basic act as a mother…breastfeeding from the breast.

I would pump and feed it to him in a bottle, but soon pumping became too much of a chore with only a hand pump. I could hardly keep up with his demands. We were low-income at the time and on the government program WIC (Woman Infants and Children), which helps supplement the diets of pregnant mothers and children who are under the age of five. They offer breastfeeding support, but I was young, exhausted, and finally took the free formula they continually offered me. I felt so much guilt over this, but I shouldn't have. Because no matter *how* my baby was getting fed, I was still feeding my baby.

When my first child was nineteen years old, his orthodontist pointed out that he has a slight tongue tie. This was the root of all his nursing and feeding problems as a baby...if only I would have known or maybe taken that breastfeeding help, it could have been caught. Nevertheless, he did grow up to be a healthy adult even without breastmilk.

In 2006, I sat in a lecture hall pregnant with my second child listening to my professor lecture about how toxic infant formula really is. I was confident I would be successful at breastfeeding this baby after an unsuccessful attempt with my first child. I was doodling flowers and butterflies in my notebook, listening, when he stated that breastmilk is toxic.

What?

I dropped my pen and stared at him, dumbfounded. Breast is best, right?

He went on to say that breastmilk is tainted by trace chemicals found in our environment. It's completely out of our control.

Well, what now?

Even my breastmilk is dirty and not pure? I guess it makes sense: chemicals from the food we eat, water we drink, and air we breathe end up in our bodies. The better we eat, the more nutritious our breastmilk will be. There are factors beyond our control in our environment that will lace our breastmilk with toxic metals and chemicals.

I sat there rubbing my giant belly full of life for the rest of class, worrying about what I was going to feed this baby. After class I stopped my professor, bombarding him with questions. He told me to stop by his office later that day so we could talk in depth about my concerns.

In his office, he had a copy of *The Omega Diet* by Artemis P. Simpoulos, MD, and Jo Robinson, which I still refer to today. He explained that there's no way around environmental factors that may taint my breastmilk, but maintaining a healthy diet is key in providing the best breastmilk for my baby. You are what you eat! He also gave me information about the La Leche League (LLL), which helps educate and support breastfeeding mothers.

Breastfeeding is best, but it may not be in the cards for you for whatever reason and it's none of anyone's business what you choose and why. Formula is not the enemy. Sometimes it's the only way a mother can get food into her baby. I know deep in my heart that every mother is trying to do the best she can with the information she has at the time, and every situation is different. Be kind, be gentle, and remember we are all forever learning, and if it makes you feel better, go get that Certified USDA Organic tattoo across your breast. Then serve it up organic-style!

MORE THAN ORGANIC FOOD

After Alexis was born, I attended our local LLL meetings. I connected with some great women through this breastfeeding support group, which changed my perspective on parenting and made a significant impact on my life.

Our group decided to meet for a picnic at a local park. It was a beautiful day…the grass was a deep green, the sky a peaceful blue, birds were singing, squirrels were scurrying about, and the air had that wonderful fresh-cut grass smell. I was happy and content to be there with my two children. It was so nice to converse with like-minded moms and other adults in general because Joe worked long hours. Things were getting better for Joe and I as he stepped into his role as a father. He was gone long hours now working on the company he had started to offer us a better life. I rarely saw him, and I was lonely.

We were all chatting and munching on our lunches when the head mom of our group, a perky blonde in a loose-fitting patchwork blouse, started a conversation about only buying organic fair-trade clothing and sheets for her children, one of whom was toddling through the grass with no diaper on because she uses the method of "elimination communication." Most of the other moms chimed in about which brands they liked best and where they bought them.

I was confused. Organic textiles? I didn't understand why you would spend the extra money on organic textiles. Children are not eating their sheets or their super cute pajamas with planets, stars, and little green-skinned extraterrestrials on them. I sat there, nodding my head and smiling at these women, feeling inadequate. I didn't fit in; I could hardly afford clothing in general, let alone the large price tag organic clothing carries with it.

I understood that organic food was important to feed your kids, but organic clothing and sheets? I thought these women were crazy, or at least so wealthy they were running out of things to spend money on.

Later that afternoon, I was walking alone with another mom who was new to the group and to the crunchy lifestyle. We discussed how we both thought these women were a bit over the top and crazy. Organic sheets? Was it really just as important as organic formula or food? I didn't dare ask for fear of judgement by these moms who I desperately needed to have in my life so I could have some adult connection.

That evening, after Alexis and Sebastian were in bed I researched this topic online and discovered that cotton is very high in pesticides, and those pesticides absorb easily into your skin when you wear cotton, especially when you sweat. These moms were onto something.

Looking back on it now, I judged them out of my own ignorance, and I was too embarrassed to admit that I was not a smart enough mom to already be privy to that information. I beat myself up over this, and it made me feel like less of a mom. I was too embarrassed to admit that I had no idea what they were talking about.

I fed my children, clothed them, and provided a happy home for them—shouldn't that have been enough? It *really* was enough, but when I saw these other moms doing more for their children than I was, I felt like I was doing it wrong.

Being a mom is hard and stressful; none of us got a manual. Even if we did, each child is so different it would have never worked. So we look to other moms and watch how they raise their children, the products they use, and the books they read. We look to each other for ideas and support. Where one mom excels, another struggles. Would I have been judged by these moms if I had told them that I didn't have organic sheets and didn't know why I needed them? Maybe. But maybe they would have taken the time to explain to me why they felt that it was important. I never gave them the chance.

HIDE THE CHEETOS

After I had been homeschooling for a few years I opened and led the first Kids for Peace chapter in our area. This nonprofit organization was started by two moms in California with a focus on empowering youth to create peace through hands-on services, global friendships, and thoughtful acts of kindness. I usually held meetings at parks and other public places, but today we were meeting at my house to put together peace packs to ship overseas.

We were a great group of like-minded moms and children, or so I thought. The children had a blast organizing items like toothbrushes, pencils, paper, small toys, and handmade inspirational cards. They stuffed these items into canvas drawstring bags adorned with colorful painted handprints from the child who stuffed it. It felt good to do good, and it seemed as if everyone was feeling the high of doing good in the world.

After the bags were completed, we headed outside for our closing parachute playtime. While the children took turns running and sitting under the parachute, I went inside to grab the snack my son and I had prepared earlier. They were adorable fruit kabobs decorated to look like caterpillars with candy eyeballs and licorice antennae, paired with boxes of organic strawberry milk.

The kids scrambled over, swarming us when they saw my son and I approaching with a tray full of fruit and a basket full of milk boxes. They had worked up an appetite with all the crafting and playing outside. I could almost hear their growling bellies. Little hands reached in eagerly, grabbing the food offered. My friend Shenoya stepped forward and with a hushed, calm voice announced, "Wait your turn, loves, there is plenty for all!"

She laughed and looked at me. "They sure are hungry. These caterpillar-kabobs are adorable. You're so clever!"

I laughed. "Not really clever," I stated. "I cannot take full credit for these cute snacks. I saw it in last month's issue of *Family Fun* magazine. I have been waiting for the right opportunity to make them."

We were interrupted by one of the boys in the group, who walked up to me after looking over the snacks and asked, "You got any chips or soda?"

"No, sorry, this is what I have for snacks today. You don't have to eat it if you don't want to," I replied.

He looked over to his mom, who gave him a stern look, snapping and pointing to the plate of caterpillar-kabobs. He turned back to me and begrudgingly grabbed one from the table nearby, then turned to sit in the grass, facing away from where I stood. Even though his eyes could not meet mine, I watched as he deconstructed the kabob, pulling apart all the fruit and leaving it on his plate. He only ate the candy eyes and licorice antenna.

After the meeting, the kids and I cleaned up plates from the yard. Some were completely empty, while others still had some fruit left, usually all of one kind. We all have our favorites, with some fruits not well liked. But there were three plates with full skewers of fruit, with only the candy missing. I assumed these were the plates of the boy and his siblings, who wanted only junk food.

I shrugged as I grabbed them, pouring them all onto one plate. "Alexis!" I shouted. "Can you come here? Take this plate of fruit and put it in the chicken pen, please. They'll be excited for their summer treat of fruit today."

She skipped over, grabbed the plate from my hand, and called out to her younger brother to come watch her place the plate in the pen. Chickens are fun to watch peck at treats. Sometimes they fight over a single grape, chasing each other through the pen as if it were the only treat, despite the fact there was an entire plate. Silly birds!

A few weeks later, this mom confessed to me that she was nervous coming over to my house. She stated that she was afraid I would judge her because she didn't eat as clean as we did. So before she came over to our house, she told her kids to clean out their van of all Cheetos bags, fast food containers, food wrappers, and to not talk about food.

She then confessed that no matter how many times she offered her children healthy options of fruits and veggies, they refused to eat them.

"So, I just give in and let them have whatever they *will* eat because I don't want them to starve," she said.

I was incredibly sad that this mom was so worried about what I would think of her that she had to prep her van and children before coming over. I have felt this too on occasion.

When she shared this with me, I laughed and explained to her that we eat junk too. I proceeded to take photos of the food currently in our cupboards. I had Jalapeño Fritos sitting next to our organic pasta sauce, Reese's peanut butter cups next to our grass-fed Epic bars, and Moose Tracks ice cream next to the organic, dye-free 100 percent fruit juice popsicles in the freezer. I explained that I too indulge in junk. We try to keep a diet of 80 percent clean food that's minimally processed, containing only whole ingredients that can be pronounced, and only some of that is even organic! The other 20 percent is eating out and letting the kids order soda with high fructose corn syrup, eating chips, experiencing the thrill of ice cream shops full of red dye, and understanding that moderation in life is what's important.

I try to model good habits by eating plenty of fruits and vegetables, but despite the fact that I fill my kids' plates with these same foods, they don't always eat them and they end up in the chicken pen. Each of my children has select veggies they will not touch, but others they enjoy (or at least stomach).

Sometimes life is not what you see at first. This mom thought I was different than I really am. What she thought I was turned out to be false. How many times have we met someone and decided we know who they are by something simple as a shirt they wear, the fast food bag in their car, or maybe the drive-thru coffee cup in their hand?

I know I have done it before. I did it when I sat at the La Leche League picnic listening to the mom talk about organic sheets.

SUPER TASTERS

So maybe you or your children cannot get past the bitter taste of some veggies. Don't beat yourself up over it. Did you know that you can be a super taster? It's real, it's a thing. Kind of a crappy superpower, though, if you ask me!

I first heard of this when my daughter was attending a large Girl Scout convention focused on earning badges. One of the workshops she signed up for was a *healthy eating* and *senses* workshop.

During the first part of this class, the instructors focused on comparing the common foods we *think* are healthy, like Bolthouse farms smoothie drinks found in the produce section of our grocery stores, to unhealthy options like a can of soda.

The smoothie drink is clearly better for you since it is made with whole fruits and veggies. The Amazing Mango flavor, my favorite, contains a whopping 260 calories and 56 grams of sugar for a 16-ounce bottle. A bottle of soda contains 200 calories and 55 grams of sugar. The instructor explained that these juice drinks are meant to be a meal replacement, not drunk alongside your meal.

The class went on, debunking many common food myths. After a conversation about how many children like veggies, they pulled out some test strips. They explained that 30 percent of the population are genetically born as super tasters. These individuals have a higher sensitivity to bitter foods like broccoli, kale, coffee, or dark chocolate.

"I'm going to pass out these strips, and when I say go, I want you to place them on your tongue, then write down what you taste," stated the instructor. "Go!"

Right away you could tell who the super tasters were. They immediately made faces and spit them out, while others just looked around, wondering what all the fuss was about.

"I don't think mine is working," a very petite scout wearing a bright pink shirt stated.

"Me either!" a small red-headed scout chimed in to say.

"Are you kidding me?" one of the older scouts shouted. "They're horrible. It tastes like soap and chemical." She went on, gagging and making weird faces before asking to head to the bathroom to rinse her mouth out.

"Everyone got the same strips," the instructor went on to say. "As you can see, they affected some of you differently. What did you taste?"

She went around the table, giving each scout the opportunity to share their reaction. They varied from three responses: revolting, slightly unpleasant, or nothing at all. Most of the answers were nothing.

While the results were shared, the moms at the back of the room were talking and sharing stories about their children's food tastes.

"It all makes sense now," stated the mom of the scout who had the strongest taste reaction to the test strips. "I have been forcing her to the point of tears to eat green veggies, and it literally tastes so much stronger to her than me. I don't particularly *love* the taste of greens, but I eat them because I know they're good for me. I have been telling my daughter to just suck it up and choke it down. I feel so bad."

We all nodded in support. Prior to this class, none of us had any idea what a super taster was.

Diving even further into the sense of taste, the instructors pulled out a tray full of lemons, sharp cheddar cheese, pickles, and vinegar.

"How would you describe the taste of these foods?"

"Sour!" an older know-it-all scout shouted.

"Yes, you are correct. But what if I told you I can change the taste of these sour foods to taste as sweet as sugar?"

"Impossible!" the same know-it-all shouted. "You can't do that. Unless you put sugar on it!"

She dug through the box in front of her and pulled out a foil packet with red lozenges nestled inside their own sealed pocket. She handed them out to everyone, even the adults, then said, "Go ahead and suck on these until they fully dissolve on your tongue."

They were not unusually sweet, salty, or sour. They tasted like a mild candy. The instructor looked around to see if people were finished, then went on to give directions.

"If you're finished with your lozenge, go ahead and grab a lemon and give it a try."

"It's gonna taste the same," the know-it-all said while my daughter's best friend, a habitual rule-follower, rolled her eyes. I saw her whisper something to my daughter as all the scouts reached for lemons.

Some dug right in with a large bite and others with just a slow lick with the tip of their tongue.

It tasted incredibly sweet. We were all disbelievers until the deep, rich sweetness of honey rolled around our mouths.

"Whoa! This is amazing," my daughter said, reaching for more.

"Don't be shy," giggled the instructor. "Go ahead and try the other foods on the tray."

We reached for the other items on the tray, all with the same result. Everything was sweet, so sweet.

So how does this work? The miracle fruit contains a chemical that affects taste receptors in the tongue. This chemical makes the tongue register sour as sweet. It's all natural, and you can find both the miracle fruit and the super taster strips on Amazon.

Or you can find links to the miracle fruit, super taster strips, and other materials in the back of this book or on my website at www.betsyharloff.com/bookresources.

Whether you feed your children organic foods or traditional foods, you are feeding them. Do your own research and choose what is best for your family. Always remember that just because you see friends posting their green smoothies and salads on their Instagram feeds, they may also have Jalapeño Fritos and Reese's cups in their cupboards too!

You know the saying, "Don't judge a book by its cover"? I'm making up a new one: "Don't judge a mom by her social media posts!"

YOU KNOW THE
SAYING,

"Don't judge a book by its cover?"

I'M MAKING UP
A NEW ONE:

"Don't judge a mom by her social media posts!"

CHAPTER 4

Saturday Morning Pancakes

One of the most primal and important jobs a parent has is feeding their kids. This seems like a very basic thing to do, but anyone who has raised a child knows this can be harder than it seems. What your kids ate for two solid weeks, they now refuse to eat, and you are stuck ripping your hair out trying to figure out what this tiny human will eat. Do you let your kid go to bed hungry because they won't eat their carrots, or do you give in and let them eat a less healthy option?

ZEN MUSIC AND BACON

Sometimes I am amazing at feeding my kids. I get up early, sizzle some pasture-raised bacon in the frying pan, whip up some rich, buttery eggs from our hens, and slice copious amounts of fresh fruit, all while sipping on organic fair-trade coffee and listening to my Zen Music and Bacon playlist on Spotify. I may even snap a photo of my amazing feat and post it on social media, because today is a good day and I am killing it at this parenting gig.

This may create the perception that this is how our mornings go every day. That I have such a picture-perfect life and only post pictures occasionally because I am too busy being perfect. Nope, I am not perfect—and if you ask me, I will tell you that I don't have it together most days. Some days I do, and those are the glorious days I want to remember. So I snap a photo and post it on social media. I don't post it so others will feel like less…I post it because I'm proud of that moment.

Back to my perfect morning…the Zen music is playing in the background, a mix of waterfalls and relaxing flutes, and I am feeling like a boss getting ready to feed my kids some superbly tasty food. The reality is that only a fraction of my five children will be as excited about this meal as I am. Some will gobble it right up; others will cry and wonder why we cannot eat gluten free donuts every day. My life will not be as picture-perfect as that Instagram photo. Truth be told, it was real food, I did cook it, it was amazing, and the Zen music was playing. But what was not as perfect was the photo of my children's reaction to the food. I didn't post that picture.

At this point I usually say something like, "This is what's for breakfast today, I will not be offering any other foods. You can choose to eat this or be hungry until lunch, but I will not be serving anything else."

This usually puts my kids into negation mode, trying to convince me that if they just eat one bite of egg, they can eat a granola bar or the YumEarth organic gummy bears that I have not-so-cleverly hidden in the back of the cupboard. As if I would allow my kids to eat gummy bears for breakfast!

Ah, but then remember: I am that amazingly perfect mother who only serves up the most wholesome food. Nope, I'm NOT the picture of perfection. I *may* have allowed my children to negotiate their way out of food before. You see, allowing it just once lets my children know loud and clear that Mom will inevitably break. This empowers my children to whine and complain! They will try relentlessly, like a lab monkey in a cage repeating similar actions in different ways to receive the result they want. They know I broke once, maybe twice, and my brilliant, persistent children will keep trying tirelessly, like that pink energizer rabbit that never stops and keeps going, and going, and going. They have more energy than me, and there are more of them. I am outnumbered.

Maybe this is a developmental milestone, but I never read about it in any of my parenting books. Let's face it, I only read parenting books in the first year to make sure all the developmental milestones were being hit. I never read about the milestones of negotiation and manipulation, but all kids learn them.

Okay, back to breakfast…I step back for a moment and notice what's really going on. It's quite amazing. My children are learning that if they keep trying, and problem-solving new ways to get what they want, they may succeed. They are learning valuable skills to use in their adult lives, that if at first you don't succeed, keep trying. Don't always accept no as an answer. I told my oldest son throughout his preteen and teen years that he will get knocked down in life more than he will ever get a helping hand up, and that one of the hardest things to learn is to keep getting up. Perseverance is the key to life, and to finding new ways to reach what most think is unattainable.

The song "Tubthumping" by Chumbawamba starts playing in my head. You know, the song that talks about getting knocked down over and over again, but that you need to keep getting up and trying again? It's one of my favorite motivational songs and can be found on my Spotify playlist mentioned at the beginning of this book.

Even in my adult life as I write this very book I keep getting knocked down:

1. Publishers do not want a first-time, inexperienced author. If you are reading this, I found a publisher or I self-published, which I was prepared to do before I started the first word because I believe in this book and its message.

2. Friends think this book has been written before by someone else. But haven't all books?

3. I'm also prepared for this book to bomb, but I hope it doesn't. I have visualized it being in the bestseller section of Barnes & Noble. But if it does bomb, I'm going to keep writing. I am prepared to write three books before I quit—but maybe after three books it will be six, then nine, and so on. I refuse to give up; I refuse to let that little voice in my head that constantly beats me down win. Ya'll know that voice, the one you hear when you are trying to do something great. That negative little sucker pops out and says things like, "You suck, you're not worthy, you'll fail, and everyone will laugh at you!" No matter how hard I try to think positively, it pops into my head.

I'm sure I also tried to get my way with my parents, which is why I persist to this day, not taking no for an answer too easily and trying new ways to reach my desired outcome. This is an evolutionary trait ensuring that roadblocks are just a way to get our brain and creative juices flowing to find new ways to overcome a situation. When my children were presented with a delicious and healthy breakfast of eggs, bacon, and fruit, they decided they didn't want it. They went into negotiation and problem-solving mode to reach the desired outcome. I should be proud!

They didn't get gluten free doughnuts or any other items they tried to negotiate for. I stood my ground. Most of my children did end up eating the delicious feast I had prepared, but a few of them just picked at it, asking for snacks an hour later, at which time I directed them to the fruit tray left over from breakfast.

SLACKER MOM MORNINGS

Let me be very clear here, not all mornings are Zen music and bacon breakfasts. Some mornings are a find-yourself-something-to-eat-and-make-it kind of morning. On these mornings, I'm not awake before my kids. They're the ones who wake me

I refuse to let
THAT LITTLE VOICE IN MY
HEAD THAT CONSTANTLY
BEATS ME DOWN WIN.
YA'LL KNOW THAT VOICE,
*the one you hear when
you are trying to do
something great.*
THAT NEGATIVE LITTLE
SUCKER POPS OUT AND
SAYS THINGS LIKE,
*"You suck, you're not
worthy, you'll fail,
and everyone will
laugh at you!"*

up on these days. If my youngest wakes up first, she climbs into my bed and asks for my phone. I groggily hand it to her and let her play games, or I haphazardly type in "YouTube" with blurry eyes and let her watch G-rated videos as I doze off for twenty minutes or so.

I really should just get up at this point, because I'm not getting any kind of quality sleep next to a kicking four-year-old who wakes me every few minutes to ask a million questions or wants to show me some neat video. But I still try to sleep, succumbing to the comfort of my warm bed. This usually happens in the winter months when I'm warm and snuggly under my covers, not yet ready to brace myself for the shock of my feet touching the cold wooden floor.

If my older children are the ones waking me up, I sometimes send them away to play video games while I sleep a little longer. Not a picture-perfect moment of parenting for sure…

Finally, I decide to drag myself out of bed, knowing that I should've been up already. My day goes much more smoothly if I'm up before the kids. That didn't happen today—I stayed up too late last night watching Netflix and I'm exhausted. I shuffle to the kitchen, boil some water in my electric kettle, then decide if it will be a coffee or tea kind of morning. I decide on coffee and scoop my favorite Starbucks Cinnamon Dolce into my French press. The smell perks me right up. I believe I like the smell of coffee more than the taste of it.

When the other children hear me in the kitchen, they flood in, eagerly awaiting food. There will be no Zen music and bacon this morning, no eggs, no fresh orange juice from the juicer. What they will have is something simple they can make or get themselves. This usually means apple-flavored organic instant oatmeal, a Kind bar, an Epic bar, fruit, or a Stonyfield's yogurt.

After I have taken a sip or two of my coffee or tea, I stand in my closet, mug in hand, and mentally go over the day and decide that I'm putting on black leggings and a loose T-shirt with a stain on the left shoulder. I don't have anywhere to go today, after all. I set my mug down on the small counter in my closet and slip into my pants.

Ahhhhh, I really love these stretchy leggings, they are so comfy.

There will be no picture posted today of my bedraggled self and my pitiful attempt at breakfast. This morning won't make it on social media, but maybe it should. Maybe when I am done with this book, I'll get back to blogging or start a podcast and start posting the not-so-picture-perfect parts of my life. Maybe by the time you read this, I will have done those things.

Did I feed my kids? Yes, which means I must be doing something right. I'm thankful to have the choice whether I make it a Zen music and bacon kind of morning or a find yourself something to eat kind of morning.

SATURDAY MORNING PANCAKES

In the spring of 2018, I started a tradition I like to call "Saturday morning pancakes." It didn't start as an every-Saturday thing at first, but it did start on a Saturday. I liked the relaxed aspect of Saturday mornings—none of my kids were playing a sport that required us to be in a rush and get out early. It was the one day out of the week that I let myself guiltlessly sleep in, then get up and make pancakes with the kids. I usually don't sleep past nine in the morning, and the kids know that if they are hungry on a Saturday, they should eat something light, like a piece of fruit. They know that soon they will be filling their bellies with delicious, butter-soaked pancakes.

Before Saturday pancakes started, I was asked many times to make pancakes, but very rarely did I say yes. Then I'd feel that heavy weight of mom guilt bearing down on me all day because I said no. Pancakes are such an ordeal! Not only are they messy, they're time-consuming. Before Saturday pancakes, I only made pancakes on holidays or special occasions, just like my father did for me when I was a child. Sometimes we really do turn into our parents, so be careful how you act. Your kids are watching, and they will inevitably take some of your habits into their adult lives.

I wasn't just making pancakes on Saturdays—we were also making memories. Some days, all five kids would be in the kitchen flipping, pouring, and cracking eggs. Sometimes Joe was there with us. Some days, it was just one of my kids. I would just try to make sure that everyone who wanted to help had a chance to lend a hand.

The pancakes are served to order—we don't all eat together. Everyone gets to eat them fresh off a nonstick ceramic pan we bought from Costco two years ago. I let them get creative with their pancakes—we've added sprinkles, chocolate chips, blueberries, strawberries, dried dates, and of course whipped cream. Unfortunately, no one has asked for kale in their pancakes yet! I did sneak freshly juiced spinach into them on St. Patrick's Day, making them a smidge healthier and a festive shade of green! Still, the multicolored, sprinkle pancakes always make the top of the list for most of my children. I don't think they taste any better, but they sure do look fun!

Another addition to the fun on Saturday mornings was the music. Although music was usually playing nonstop in the kitchen, on Saturdays it's a little bit louder and usually involves dancing. We would often listen to soundtracks from Disney movies like *Frozen, Home,* and *Moana.* I am a lover of most music, so I'm usually quite flexible on genre, I just like the beats!

Saturdays are some of my favorite mornings. I know I'll be making pancakes, so it really helps me plan my time and not stress about the extra mess of kids helping in the kitchen. From start to clean-up, the whole Saturday morning pancake ritual usually takes about two hours. This is easily accomplished on mornings I've planned for it, but is not so easy on a whim.

To make things even smoother on pancake Saturdays, I do some prep work the night before, getting out bowls, measuring spoons, and other kitchen tools. It only takes a few minutes to stage the kitchen in preparation for delicious pancakes, and the kids sometimes like to help in the kitchen after we clean up from dinner the night before. I think the anticipation makes them love Saturday morning pancakes even more. After all, what's not to love about a fluffy, butter-soaked, moist, cake-like breakfast concoction covered in real maple syrup?

What started as a specific day to cook a time-consuming breakfast treat turned into so much more. This day of the week has come to be a favorite of mine, not because of the food but because of the memories. For so many years, I found myself cooking in the kitchen with a baby on my hip, a toddler tugging at my leg, and a slightly older child begging to cook with me because it looked fun. I couldn't teach her; I was overwhelmed just getting hot food into hungry mouths during this chaotic season of motherhood. I was hardly holding it together!

Now my children are older and we can have great conversations while we cook, sing, dance, laugh, and create crazy concoctions that may or may not be edible. This day is more than just food; it's creating memories to last a lifetime.

CAKE FOR BREAKFAST

After every birthday celebration comes "cake for breakfast," when we eat the leftover cake, and it's one of Joe's biggest pet peeves of my parenting.

"This is your worst idea ever," Joe says the morning after every single birthday. "There is so much sugar in that cake. This is a horrible food to give our kids first thing in the morning."

This is rather unusual, because I'm usually the one in the house looking to reduce sugar and making sure the kids are eating a healthy diet. We eat pretty good all year: no sodas, limited juice, and only breakfast cereals that contain less than 2 grams of sugar per serving. Meanwhile, my husband chugs can after can of Dr. Pepper and eats Golden Grahams, which contain 9 grams of sugar per a three-quarter-cup serving. But for some reason, the thought of me giving our kids leftover cake for breakfast really gets under his skin. I don't get it! Two frosted donuts with sprinkles have the same amount of sugar as a small slice of cake. Yet donuts are an acceptable breakfast food—and they're usually paired with orange juice, which has more sugar than a can of soda. But still, my husband despises that I feed our children cake for breakfast.

How did I come up with the idea? The answer is rather simple. If my children know cake is in the house, they will ask me a hundred times if they can have it. "Just a small bite...a small taste, pretty please," they'll beg. This will go on all day long, despite the fact that I already told them it will be served after dinner.

Recently, a mom on Instagram mentioned in a post that her kids were enjoying leftover cake for breakfast while she read a book and sipped on her coffee. Comments flooded this post from moms stating they have the same feast the morning after a birthday or celebration that served cake. I couldn't believe my eyes, I was not alone!

For me, cake for breakfast means I can get that out of the way nice and early, so I don't have to listen to my children begging for cake all day long. In fact, my daughter said to me after the last birthday, "You know, sometimes it's no fun celebrating birthdays for my siblings because I am not getting any presents, but then I remember I'm getting cake for breakfast in the morning and I'm so excited."

What started as a way for my kids to not bother me about eating cake quickly turned into an exciting tradition for all to enjoy—except Joe. He passionately hates this tradition and rolls his eyes every post-birthday morning.

They're going to eat the cake as leftovers no matter what, and it's the same amount of sugar whether it's eaten at eight in the morning or eight in the evening. And if it's eaten early in the morning, they have a chance to burn off all those extra calories. So why *not* eat cake for breakfast?

MADDI'S FRIDGE

I recently read the book *Maddi's Fridge* by Lois Brandt to my four-year-old. The book was on our library's "101 Picture Books" challenge list. My nine-year-old son saw me grabbing the book from the stack we had just checked out and said, "This is a really good one, Mom. Bailey will like it."

"What's it about?"

"There are these two girls who play at the playground together, and one realizes that the other girl has no food in her fridge and is hungry, so she tries to help her out but keeps messing up."

When I was twenty-four years old, on welfare, and struggling as a new mom, I often wondered what I was going to feed my child that day. I would wake up in the morning, investigate my empty fridge, and try to figure out what I would feed my one-year-old, myself, and his father.

I was too proud to ask for help from my parents. They already knew I was on welfare, but the food assistance I was getting was not enough for fresh meats, fruits, veggies, and highly nutritious things. That's the choice many parents must make. Do I buy healthy fresh foods? Or do I buy cheaper options that have little to no nutrition, but fill their hungry bellies?

One morning when Sebastian was still a baby, I asked my parents to come over and watch their beloved first and only grandchild. I had an appointment for my yearly checkup at the gynecologist. I never miss those appointments, because I knew a mom who skipped them for five years, and when she finally went, she found out she had stage 4 cervical cancer.

My parents must have been appalled at the sight of my empty fridge—it looked just like Maddi's in the story. One of them stayed at my apartment with Sebastian while the other went grocery shopping while I was at the doctor's office, completely unaware. When they left, they didn't even tell me what they did, but instead hid the food and left without saying a word about it.

A few hours after they were gone, I felt that familiar pang of hunger. I opened my fridge, thinking it was empty. But to my great surprise, I found cartons of fresh juice, whole milk, loads of fresh fruits and veggies, pork chops, cheese of all types, fresh chicken breasts, ground beef, cube steak, and delicious, individually wrapped cheesecake bars that were much too pricey for me to ever consider buying. My freezer contained even more vegetables, a variety of cuts of meat, chicken nuggets, fish sticks, seasoned fish fillets, ice cream, and Dove chocolate ice cream bars. Those were my mom's favorite, so I figured she had left my dad to watch Sebastian and bought all this delicious food to fill my kitchen. My cupboards were full of canned soups, dry pasta, marinara, oatmeal, cereal, fruit snacks, and granola bars.

It took so much self-restraint to resist ripping open dozens of packages and diving face-first into all this food. There were so many scrumptious treats, things I would have never spent money on. I am proud to say that I held it together and didn't dive into all the delicious goodness. I did, however, rip open one of those cheesecake bars and indulge in its silky sweet goodness, savoring every single bite and letting it roll around in my mouth before I swallowed it. When I finished licking the cheesecake wrapper, I called my parents to thank them.

That was the worst it ever got, but I will never forget the awful feeling of wondering what I would feed myself or my children, or the joy of seeing my empty fridge filled to capacity with so much food.

In 2012, I did my first juice fast/cleanse. During those seven days, I consumed a copious amount of fresh juice. I was hungry the whole time—the person who said you won't be hungry during a juice fast is the same liar who said you'll forget all about the pain of childbirth when you first hold your baby.

Still, no matter how hungry I got, I knew my body was getting massive amounts of micronutrients from the juices, even if my brain was telling my stomach I was starving! Fresh juice was helping my body detoxify from heavy metals and nourish my cells.

Those hungry nights, when my belly rumbled and roared, became some of my most spiritual nights. I would lay there thinking about women around the world who were in their beds with the same ache, but actually starving and wondering how they were going to feed their families. I realized how lucky and blessed I really am. I believe this is why some religions fast—when you are hungry on purpose, it really makes you think about those who have less than you and are in far worse situations. How many moms are hungry tonight...like, legit hungry?

> *"A mother is a person who, seeing there are only four pieces of pie for five people, promptly announces she never did care for pie."*
>
> **—TENNEVA JORDAN**

WATERMELON AND POPCORN: IT'S WHAT'S FOR DINNER!

I was eight months pregnant with my fourth child, living in a house with no air conditioning during one of the hottest summers I could remember. Heat is not my friend—I have neurocardiogenic syncope and am prone to passing out when overheated. On top of that, I am ghostly white and get sun poisoning from the slightest amount of sun exposure. Ironically, sitting oceanside with a good book and an ice-cold drink is my happy place, but I need to be covered up and under an umbrella. Anyhow, back to the summer of hell...

The clock had just struck 4 p.m., and we were entering the witching hour. In our house, the witching hour was more like a witching window; it started around four in the afternoon when the children were tired and beginning to get hungry. Guess what? I was tired too! I was eight months pregnant and pouring sweat. It was over 100°F in the house, and every time I moved, I would get Braxton Hicks contractions so severe I doubled over in pain. My only saving grace was the single window A/C unit in our bedroom, but I only turned that on at night so I could sleep as peacefully and comfortably as possible in a small 12'x12' room with three kids, our beloved black lab, and my husband. It was a tight squeeze, but it was cool and so it was divine. We made it work.

On this particular day, it wasn't bedtime yet, and the kids and I were hot, tired, cranky, and bored. I had planned on making chicken fajitas for dinner, but the thought of all that sautéing and chopping in my sweltering kitchen did not sound appealing. I was the only one who would eat it anyhow. Everyone else would just want cheese and soft corn tortillas, so why bother? I gave it some thought, rummaged through the kitchen, and came up with a new dinner plan that would please everyone except Joe, who was rarely home anyway. He had started a new business a few years before that provided software for mystery shopping companies and spent most of his waking moments trying to lift his company off the ground.

I pulled out a large stockpot, scooped in three tablespoons of coconut oil, turned up the heat, and yelled, "Who wants to help make popcorn?"

The kids all raced in to help, and by "help" I really mean dumping in the corn kernels and watching the popcorn pop through the pot's glass lid.

"Are we eating popcorn?" squealed my children, excited about this fun dinner choice and looking like they'd just won the lottery.

"Yes," I replied, smiling at their eager little faces.

"Yay!" they cheered in unison.

While they happily munched on popcorn, I cut up slices of watermelon for a thirst-quenching side dish. There's nothing more refreshing than fresh slices of watermelon on a hot summer's day.

Just as I was serving the last of the watermelon slices, my childhood best friend called. She didn't have any children and worked nights in the same bar where we used to work together.

"Hey, whatcha doing?" she said.

"I just finished up dinner."

"Oooooh, what did you make? I'm at a loss for ideas tonight."

I laugh and say, "I'm sure you'll not want to make what I served for dinner."

When I explained what I made for dinner, she was appalled. She later laughed about my summer choice with her husband, and they joked for years about my watermelon and popcorn dinner.

"Just wait until you have your own children," I said. "You may find yourself serving your kids some random foods because you don't want to slave over the stove that day and have your kids refuse to eat it."

Ten years later, watermelon and popcorn for dinner is still a running joke between us. That best friend of mine now has a four-year-old of her own. She called me one evening to let me know that I was an amazing mom and a genius. She hadn't fed her child watermelon and popcorn for dinner, but she now understood the plight of cooking a big meal and making a mess of the kitchen, only to have her child refuse to eat it. Her husband works second shift, so it's usually just her son and her eating dinner. She told me that some days she just runs to McDonald's and grabs her child dinner, then stops at Panera to get herself a soup and salad combo.

You don't always need to feed your children a traditional dinner. Some out-of-the-box thinking and creativity will fill your kids' bellies and add a whimsical element to the day.

ICE CREAM DINNER

Although the watermelon and popcorn for dinner is still on the healthy (ish) spectrum of food choices, having ice cream for dinner really is not. At least once every summer, on a day we had a late lunch or when the summer heat has spoiled our appetites, I surprise my children with ice cream for dinner. Depending on my mood and forethought, we either stop at a local ice cream shop—our favorite being Mr. G's Barn—or I pull out some Turkey Hill Natural ice cream from the deep freezer. I lay out chopped nuts, sprinkles, fruit, chocolate chips, coconut flakes, and whipped cream to create a sundae bar. Then, to make things even sillier, we have dinner for dessert, making it a fun backward summer meal.

I try my best to make sure my kids are eating healthy, nutritious foods and setting them up with good habits they can take into adulthood, but sometimes this mom thing is just really hard and you have to let go of all your preconceived notions about what a good parent really is. Stop staring at those social media pictures of perfect lives and just know that we are all human and flawed.

We are living this life the best way we can, and we are bound to make mistakes. If fact, by making those mistakes, we all become better parents.

I am not perfect, I am insanely flawed. I don't serve kale and grass-fed beef every day—sometimes we eat at Chick-fil-A. Okay, a lot of times we eat at Chick-fil-A. In fact, we save Chick-fil-A sauce in our fridge for the days I make frozen, gluten-free dino nuggets at home.

At the end of the day, what really matters is that your children were fed. Did they go to sleep in a warm bed with full bellies? Did they go to sleep loved? Then you're doing a good job. I wholeheartedly believe that every mom is doing the best she can with the information she has. When I look at myself at age twenty-three as a first-time mom, compared to my present age of forty-two with five children ages 5–19, I see that I have grown and changed immensely. Am I perfect now? Hell no! Do I have it all together? No again. I know more than I did when I was twenty-three, but I'm still learning and growing as a person and a parent.

I wholeheartedly believe

THAT EVERY MOM

IS DOING THE BEST

SHE CAN

with the information she has.

CHAPTER 5

The Hot Mess Mama

I think most of us wander around all day feeling like a hot mess. Some days we look like it too! Hair is unwashed and in a messy bun or ponytail because you have yet to figure out how to make the messy bun look messy but also neat and purposeful, like your friends in their social media posts. You're wearing yoga pants covered in boogers and snot from your little ones who snuggle their faces against your leg while you're trying to cook dinner. You have on a T-shirt with spit-up stains on the right shoulder, and your house has sticky fingerprints on all the windows, TV stands, and walls...but YOU are still a superstar mama!

YOU are the most amazing person in your children's eyes. Don't talk down about yourself—they're watching and learning from everything you do. Smile, laugh, and enjoy the moment, because all too soon your house will be clean and empty, no longer full of small children, and you'll miss those days dearly. Your children don't care if you have mastered the messy bun or if you're still in your pajamas. They care if you're happy, because if you're happy they will be too!

My oldest is nineteen now, and the time flew by faster than a speeding bullet. One day I was pushing him on the black toddler swing at the park, exhausted by his requests to push him higher.

Now he's a man who just signed a lease for his first apartment. He has his own journey ahead of him—I gave him the building blocks, and he's going to stack, sort, tear down, and build the life he wants.

Having one child who is nineteen and one who is five puts me in a unique position because I have seen how fast it goes. I cherish those moments with my younger children even more now. Have I raised all my children the same? No! I have changed and grown. No one is perfect; we are all struggling in our own way with our own stuff. Our struggles may not look the same, but that doesn't make them any less of a struggle.

At age forty-two, I feel like I may have just figured life out…sort of. I look back at the thirty-year-old me, the twenty-year-old me, and the sixteen-year-old me and I see how much I have grown and changed. I'm sure when I hit fifty, I will look back at my forty-two-year-old self and think I was so young back then and knew so little.

I think us parents are all a bit of a hot mess, in varying degrees. I believe we're all struggling. How could we not be? Children came into our lives with no instruction booklet and changed us in ways we had never dreamed of. For me, it was the moment I saw my miracle baby look back at me with his squinty eyes adjusting to the bright, harsh world. He was so new and raw. The world around us blurred—the only sight perfectly in focus was his face. We were surrounded by doctors and medical staff, both grandmas, and Joe, but I couldn't see them. I couldn't hear them. The only thing I saw was him, my firstborn, my rough draft, the one I made the most mistakes with, the one who changed me forever. I knew holding my nine-pound, eleven-ounce baby boy that my life would never be the same.

Over the next few days, my heart grew and filled with more love than I had ever imagined it could. My heart also filled with worry. I worried if he was eating enough; I worried if he was sleeping enough; I worried if his bowel movements were okay. I investigated the future and worried about his life and if it would be good. This tiny human was completely dependent on me. Then, in a whirlwind of memories, all my rebellious teenage years came crashing back to me and my heart broke. It broke for my parents.

I was a rebellious child, a high school dropout, a runaway, a moving train jumper, and a law-breaker. The only reason I didn't spend a large amount of time behind bars is because I rarely got caught. I once spent fifteen minutes in a sticky, oozy, smelly garbage can with who knows what crawling inside to avoid being arrested. I heard the officer walk next to the can and say on his radio, "Clear, the culprit is not behind the house. She must have jumped the fence. Circle around to the north and look for her there." Another time I fell asleep in the cold under a car in some random neighborhood while police searched for me.

How could I have done this to my parents?

I looked down, teary-eyed, at my sweet baby boy and thought about how it would tear me apart if my own child did this to me. I was already so worried about him and he was only days old! How could I possibly worry more? I grabbed the phone to call my mom.

"Hello?" she answered in her usual upbeat, cheery tone.

"Does worrying about your child ever stop? Does it get better? Does it go away?" I asked her.

"No, honey, it doesn't. I worry about you now just as much as I did when you were a baby," she said in a low voice.

She was sad for me, her own heart breaking over my realization of the heaviness of motherhood.

"Oh!" I pause for a moment, then say, "I'm sorry for all my reckless ways as a teenager, for everything I put you through. I had no idea what this would do to you…how could I know? If I did, I would've never done it. Well, maybe I would've if I am being honest, but I am truly sorry."

Motherhood changed so much in me. I always knew I was strong, but I had no idea of what the word "strong" really meant as a mother.

A strong mom goes hungry to feed her kids.

A strong mom makes friends with people she doesn't like because their kids are friends.

A strong mom must let go when she wants to hold her children the tightest.

A strong mom does things she is terrified of doing.

A strong mom doesn't shower for days because she doesn't want her baby to cry when she sets them down.

A strong mom also sets that baby down to cry for fifteen minutes for a quick shower.

A strong mom bites her tongue and knows that not every battle is hers to fight.

A strong mom also speaks up and says what is on her mind. It can take just as much courage to hold your tongue as it does to speak up.

A strong mom says no.

A strong mom also says yes.

The word "strong" is subjective. We are all different and lead very different lives. Strong looks different for each mom. We're all on this motherhood journey together, but not always on the same path, and that's okay.

In the literal sense of being strong, mamas rock that too! Sometimes I wonder how so many of us have that out-of-shape "mom body" because it takes great strength to cook dinner one-handed with a baby on your hip. Ever try to collapse a double stroller one-handed because you are holding your toddler's hand next to a busy street with an infant strapped to your back? A day at the park always seems like a great idea, until I get there with my little kids and find myself lifting them in and out of swings, pushing them higher and higher, going down the slide together, and playing freeze tag. The physical demands of motherhood can be exhausting at first, but with each year that passes, it gets less and less exhausting. Children grow more and more independent and eventually spend more time away from you.

This is where I think grandparents may have it made, because they still remember those exhausting days with their now-grown children and realize how important those moments really were. They cherish the moments with their grandchildren, remembering the exhausting days of early parenting. They live fully in the moment and know they will be sore and tired the next day, slathering on the Tiger Balm to soothe sore muscles and soaking in an Epsom salt bath with a cup of herbal tea.

The hardest parenting years for me were when I had an infant, a nineteen-month-old, a three-year-old, and an eight-year-old. Joe worked long hours building the business that he eventually sold, so he was never home. Those days of solo-parenting four children are a bit of a blur. I was so sleep-deprived, yet tried to be strong physically and mentally for my children. It left me completely drained.

I should've asked for more help; I should've taken more breaks; I should've practiced more self-care instead of just surviving each day. I thought I could do it all, and I did, but at the cost of looking back at pictures and not even remembering them. I struggled, but I held it together because I wanted a large family. I feared asking for help because I didn't want to hear what I most feared: "Why did you have that many children if you can't handle it?"

Looking back, I don't think anyone would have said that. It was just my own thoughts taunting me. Asking for help shows weakness, I told myself, and I'm not weak—I'm strong! But what I know now is that being strong means asking for help and knowing your limitations. That was a hard lesson to learn, and only at age forty-two have I really learned it. I am STRONG when I take it all on, but I am STRONGER when I ask for help.

Learn from my mistakes, mama…take that break, ask for help, and don't run yourself ragged.

Asking for help
shows weakness,
I TOLD MYSELF, AND I'M
NOT WEAK—
I'm strong!
BUT WHAT I KNOW NOW
IS THAT BEING STRONG
MEANS

Asking for help
and knowing your
limitations.

CHAPTER 6

The Mom Ride

Whether you have a twelve-passenger van, a minivan, an SUV, or a small car, you should be able to relate to the mom ride! When you cart little people around in your vehicle, you need snacks, unless you can drive with screaming children. Children like to be fed often, and if they're bored—like on car rides—they want food to entertain them. Or maybe that's just when they realize they're hungry, because they're no longer focused on all the things running through their little minds.

Every few months, I clean my van of all the waffle fries, crumbs, sucker sticks, fruit pouches, juice box straws, dry cereal, pretzels, and if I'm lucky, the occasional piece of gum or gummy bear making everything a gooey mess. I enlist the children's help because they had a part in this dump site. They love to help when the shop vac is involved, but are never too thrilled about gathering all the items that have accumulated in the van and putting them away in the house, including all the toys, socks, past-due library books, rocks gathered from hikes, and maybe even a single shoe. Who leaves a van wearing only one shoe? And how did I not notice?

I'm not innocent either. I yell at the kids for leaving trash in the car, only to find a few Starbucks cups in the front seat, along with an empty kombucha bottle and a Reese's peanut butter cup wrapper.

I cannot count the number of times I've gotten into a friend's car and she'll say something like, "Don't mind the mess!"

I always laugh and say, "You do know that I have five kids!" My van is a wreck. I'm constantly cleaning it. Every mom I've met over the last nineteen years of parenting has a messy car—except for one.

MEET MICHELLE

She has five kids, just like me. Her kids range in age from a baby to a preteen, and she drives a white Subaru Forester. She's constantly running her kids to and from events and activities, always on the go and always late. We were recently at Maumee Bay State Park camping with a group of friends when one of my children kept complaining she was cold. "I have an extra blanket in the car," she says, looking at me. "I can go get it."

"Sure," I say and follow her to her car. As she hits the button on her key to raise the trunk, I can almost hear angels singing, and there may have been a light shining down from the heavens to fully illuminate her immaculate trunk. It was like nothing I'd seen before. There were two thick falsa blankets neatly stacked on the left side of her trunk. On the right was a square black metal basket with neatly organized snacks and disinfectant wipes, and not a crumb or speck of dust to be found.

"Did you just clean your car?" I ask in pure astonishment.

She grins, cocks her head to the side like a confused dog, and replies, "Um...no. Why do you ask?"

"Well..." I pause. "Your car is so clean, like amazingly clean! I've never in my life seen a mom who has as many kids as us, even less than us, with a car this clean."

She chuckles, handing me the blanket. As she closes the trunk, I shove my head inside to get a better look. "Is your entire car this immaculate?" I ask, in complete bewilderment.

"Yeah…mostly," she says. "I spend so much time in my car that I keep it very clean. It makes me angry to get into a dirty car!"

"Wow! Kudos to you, mama, I want a clean car too, but I just can't keep up. I just don't have the time."

Which is a lie. I think back to the TED talk by Laura Vanderkam where she talked about time management. She said there is no such thing as no time, but there is a thing called "not a priority"!

I immediately feel bad. How is this mom, who has as many kids as me, keeping her car this clean? But it all comes down to priorities.

Here's the thing, mamas, we all have the same twenty-four hours in each day. How we choose to spend those hours is entirely up to us. This mama made having a clean car a priority. Clearly, it is not a priority to me. I clean my van out every few months when it gets so gross that I can't stand it anymore.

We need to stop comparing ourselves to other mamas, but this is so much easier said than done. Their wins don't make the rest of us failures. We all are truly great at something, but we can't be awesome at everything. The best thing you can do for yourself every night before you go to bed is list all the things you DID get done. Write it out, look at it, and be proud. Don't focus on what you DID NOT get done. That's a waste of time and energy. Just because Michelle has a clean car doesn't mean she made a home-cooked dinner that night. Maybe she got her kids take-out from their favorite fast food joint. Sure, my van was a mess, but I spent over an hour making a home-cooked meal. We all have different priorities, and that's okay.

Neither of these situations make us a better parent—we are just juggling this mom job differently. Her picture-perfect car doesn't make her a better mom, any more than my picture-perfect home-cooked meal makes me a better mom. And just so you don't think I make home-cooked meals every night, think back to the waffle fries in my van—they came from Chick-fil-A! I'm not perfect…none of us are. We have our picture-perfect, Instagram moments, and our bad ones as well.

ROTTEN CHICKEN IN THE VAN

It was that time of year again—the quarterly cleaning of the van. But this time was different. This time, we were going to wash the van too! The kids filled buckets of water with soap, dipped large yellow sponges in, and then scrubbed. I even splurged on some Mrs. Meyers lilac-scented all-purpose cleaner to bring that fresh spring scent into the van. Usually we clean with just vinegar water and essential oils, but not that day. I wanted the sweet flowery scent of spring, and I just love the smell of lilacs.

A few days after we were done, the middle boys who sit in the very back row were complaining that it smelled like a fart. I ignored them because usually that means they are literally farting and yelling about it...the joy of boys! But a few days later, as I was grabbing something out of the middle row, I got a whiff of the fart smell and it was BAD!

"What's that smell?" I ask.

"That's what we've been trying to tell you, it smells back here... BAD!" they reply.

"Well, did you leave anything wet in the car?"

"Here're my socks. They were wet a few days ago, but they're dry now," Xander said, handing me his crumpled socks.

"Eeeeeew, it must be the socks, please do not leave them in the van," I said, throwing the socks into a garbage bag and planning to just buy new socks.

I thought I had solved the smell issue, but the very next day I was almost knocked back by the smell when I opened the van door.

"I just cleaned the van, what could possibly smell this horrendous?"

The kids piled into the car, gagging.

"I know it smells," I said. "As soon as we get back home, we are pulling everything out of the van to figure out what that noxious odor is."

We arrived home from the library an hour later, and I started pulling everything out of the van. After seeing there was nothing in the main part of the van, I walked around to the back. As soon as the tailgate lifted, I was hit with a thick, invisible miasma.

"Holy mother of stink! What are you boys doing back here? This is horrible!" I shouted, gagging.

My boys just laughed. "We tried to tell you! It's BAD!"

I picked up a blue and orange striped picnic blanket that I kept in the trunk and immediately saw the source of the stink: a white foam tray full of raw, very rotten chicken breasts. The last time I was at the store had been well over a week before, just after we had cleaned out the van. I thought I had bought chicken breasts, but when the kids unloaded the groceries, the package must have slipped under the picnic blanket. Thank goodness this didn't happen in the middle of summer, because if one fly had made it in there, I would have had a van full of maggots...ew!

The blankets and the trunk carpet reeked, despite scrubbing with vinegar and water. After dousing the carpet with an entire bottle of tea tree essential oil, I pulled the van around so the carpet would be hit with the sanitizing power of the sun! After a couple days of repeated scrubbing and sun exposure, the van no longer smelled like a rank mix of rotten chicken and tea tree oil.

BODY WORK

When Sebastian was just eight years old, we lived in a small house in the city with a small driveway. We had just upgraded from my four-door Mercury Sable—the engine blew because in the four years I owned it, I never, ever, not even once had the oil changed. I was preoccupied, and I thought it was optional maintenance. Lesson learned!

Instead, we had just purchased a silver Dodge Caravan. To this day, this is the only vehicle I've ever owned that was brand-spanking new off the lot, complete with that new car smell. We were expecting baby number four, so we needed something bigger anyhow.

It was a nice spring day, and Sebastian wanted to go outside and ride his bike. I decided to stay in the house and play with the little ones. I explained to him that he could ride his bike up and down the short driveway and down the street for three houses down on either side of our house. His bike had seen better days—it had logged lots of playing by my little boy. The black rubber grips on both handlebars were cracked on the ends, exposing the metal underneath. As Sebastian rode his bike down the driveway, he accidentally swerved a little too close to the new van and scraped the metal handle along the entire side of the van. I was pretty mad, but Joe was livid!

We had four kids—they're going to make mistakes and break a lot of things. Children are expensive because of all the things they damage, break, and destroy. Some of the things my children have done over the years are:

1. Shatter a window with a golf ball.
2. Put my driver's license, credit cards, and a few gift cards down the heat vent. They are all still there, by the way, and we currently have renters in that house. Someday they will be found.
3. Break the glass on the front of the oven with a perfectly placed hit from a ceramic mug.
4. Color on my freshly painted beige walls with red and black Sharpies. That artwork stayed there for two years until we needed to paint it so we could rent out the house. Every time I tried to scrub it off, the eco-friendly, no-VOC paint would come off, but the black marker stayed, so it stayed!
5. Using acrylic paint on the kitchen table with no newspaper under it.

I have found ways to cut costs on general needs like food, clothing, and education. I had to, after my children broke so many things. We shop at thrift stores for clothing, hit up end-of-season clearance sales, and always look out for sales.

Children are going to break and damage things. There's no way around that; it's all part of the learning process. That is why you are there to guide, teach, and shape these little people. You can't expect them to learn without making mistakes. I would rather my children actively play outside, exploring the limitations of what their growing bodies can do, than sit inside all day in a bubble. If you happen to pull up next to me on the road only to notice my scratched van, peer inside and you will notice my van full of kids. Or maybe you're walking down my street and notice chalk drawings covering the side of my house and a boarded-up window. You will know children live here. We are making memories and learning along the way.

CARWASH

My name is Betsy, and I have never driven into an automatic car wash. There, I said it. I have taken my kids once or twice before, but I switched seats with my husband so he could drive in. I have been driving since I was sixteen, but I was afraid I wouldn't drive on the track right or fail to put it in neutral at the correct time, messing up the whole machine!

We passed an automatic car wash not too long ago, and my kids asked what it was. I told them, and they were super excited to try it. Months ticked by, and I was often reminded of my promise to take my kids to the car wash. Finally, the day arrived. We were heading to the park just after my first writing conference, and I was feeling positive after getting great feedback on this book.

"Can we go to the car wash today?"

"Sure, we'll swing by after we leave the park."

As we approached the large beige building, the kids squealed when they saw the green turtle logo. But I was dealing with a different emotion: *fear!*

We pulled up to the flashy ordering screen listing my options. There was the Rain Shower for five dollars, the Tropical Storm for ten dollars, or the Hurricane for fifteen dollars. I had already decided on the Hurricane when the kids started chanting, "Hurricane, do the Hurricane wash!"

The whole process looked completely automated: push the button for the wash you want and insert your cash or credit card... but then what? I saw a young man in a green polo shirt. He was about Sebastian's age. "Hey, excuse me," I yelled, waving. "Can I get some help?"

I explained that I had never done this before. He chuckled, then walked me through the process, starting with payment. I didn't need help with that part, but I didn't say anything; I just smiled and gratefully accepted. After payment was received, I was told to continue driving around to the opening of the wash doors. My heart was racing as I pulled around, hoping that I didn't miss the track. He waved me forward like an airplane runway traffic controller.

"Now shift to neutral!" he yelled over the loud machines spraying water and soap.

The van jerked in a side-to-side motion. My eyes got big as I looked to make sure things were okay. The kids were already squealing with excitement as he shouted, "Have fun!" Then he ran over, handed me suckers for the kids, and gave me a smile and a thumbs-up.

We started rolling into the car wash, and I panicked. My window was still down. Oh, how entertaining that would have been, to be sprayed with soap and water! I took a deep breath and tried to relax as the kids excitedly pressed their noses to the windows for an even closer view. They hooted and hollered as the car was pelted with jets of water. Then came the attack of large alien-like tentacles sliding across the van. Then streams of multicolored foaming solvents squirted our vehicle. I looked into the rearview mirror, smiling at the astonishment on their faces with each blast. To be completely honest, it was kinda cool, and I was feeling a little like a kid myself!

When we were halfway through, I finally felt my muscles relax, knowing that I had conquered a fear. It was a simple, small, irrational fear, but it was a fear! I sat there smiling, enjoying the giggles and squeals of excitement. I could see the light at the end of the tunnel—and not just from the end of the car wash, but a light deep within me, because I had conquered a fear and it felt so good!

Despite the fact that I had conquered my fear of the automatic car wash, I have not returned, mainly because I feel fifteen dollars is a lot of money to spend on washing a vehicle. That's three trips to Starbucks, which a lot of people feel is a waste of money, but we all have our crutches.

The outside of the van gets dirty fast. My kids love to draw faces and words on the van when there is snow, ice, rain, mud, and dried salt from a Midwest winter. We also live on a farm, with a long gravel driveway leading back to our house. No matter how many dark gray Honda Odysseys there are—and there are plenty—I can always find mine because it's the one coated in grime. My van looks like a Suzuki Samurai that went mudding, except that I just drove down my driveway and went to the grocery store. On hot summer days, I let my kids play in the hose and wash the van while they're at it. The end result never turns out as great as a car wash, but they have fun helping out.

I posted a picture on Facebook about a year back showing my van after my child "washed" it. What he really did was smear rain around on the car, so when it dried, the car was covered with muddy child-sized swirls. I thought this was cute and funny, so I posted it on social media next to all the other posts of the perfectly washed, shiny, and waxed cars!

CHAPTER 7

Where's Waldo?

Throughout my twenty years of parenting, I have lost children three times, forgotten a child in a car once, and thought a child was stolen from my house. This may seem like a lot, but like I have stated many times before, I'm not perfect. I want all of you who are struggling and failing to know that you are not alone. YOU ARE NOT ALONE! Do you hear me? We all struggle and make mistakes. Parenting is not an exact science, and if you have more than one child then you already know. Just when you think you have this parenting thing figured out, the next kid comes along and everything changes.

In this chapter, you will read about my most frightening moments as a parent, the moments when I realized that one small mistake could have changed everything. During every moment in the chapter, I may have looked like I was holding it together, but I was an absolute wreck, with my heart racing, blood pressure rising, blinking back tears, trying to stop my hands from shaking, and ignoring the urge to vomit.

When talking with other moms about my experiences, they have shared moments just like mine. They were hiding these stories as well, maybe out of fear of being judged. It was only when I told friends that I was writing a book about parenting failures and my "big mistakes" that they opened up and shared a few of their stories. I have included two of these stories. So, let's jump right in, shall we?

2015 FREE RANGING CHILD

It was a beautiful day at the Toledo Zoo, 75 degrees and sunny. The animals were especially active and enjoying the cooler day, just like us. We rode the train through the African safari, then hopped on the carousel and laughed as we went around—it was a magical day. We have one of the top zoos in the country, and it has expanded many times over the years. Because of this, the zoo is now separated by a highway so you have to take a bridge over the highway to get to the other half, or take the newly restored tunnel underneath. We were heading back to the car, walking up a ramp that leads across a bridge to the other side of the Toledo Zoo. I had all five children with me; my youngest was an infant. My most independent child, Xander, was seven. He liked to run ahead and always pushed the limits on how far he could go, asserting his independence.

When we reached the top of the ramp, Xander was not there. I was a little worried, but not too much. We went to the zoo often, so he knew his way around. Also, I often let the kids run ahead across the bridge and meet me at the bottom.

At the halfway point, however, I started to get worried. I sent my two older children ahead to see if Xander was at the bottom of the ramp. They said he wasn't. I started to panic. I asked one of my kids to stay on one side of the ramp while I ran back to the other side to see if we missed him somehow.

I ran back pushing the stroller and trailing a few of my kids. He was not there...he was GONE. Images flashed through my mind of him being shoved into the trunk of a car and hauled off. What if I never saw him again?

I might vomit.

I tasted the bile in my throat. I was in a full panic, but trying to hold it together for my other children. I called my husband

and told him that I'd lost our child. I'm not sure why I called him—moral support maybe, hoping he might calm me down. But he was at work and couldn't talk long. I don't even recall what we said. Then I hung up and raced to find a zoo worker to let them know I had lost a child.

What kind of shitty mom loses her child?

"I lost my child," I said, looking at the worker with tears filling my eyes.

"Is your child Xander?" he asked.

"YES! YES! YES!" I eagerly said, blinking back the tears.

He's safe.

I was mad at him. I was mad at me. How could I let this happen?

Thankfully, I always taught my children that if they were lost, they should find a person in uniform or find a mom with children and ask her for help. I read somewhere when I had only one child that statistically, if you find a female who has kids with her, she would be the safest option.

I didn't yell when I saw Xander. I could tell he was terrified, and I hoped this might curb a bit of his independence. And it did. Years later, he's still very headstrong and independent, but he remembers that moment with clarity.

UNCAGED ANIMALS

I was at our beloved zoo yet again with my friend and her children…we spend a lot of time there. Between the two of us, we had eight children. We were inside one of the children's buildings. It had hands-on activities and a great indoor play space with fake trees that had holes to hide in, a log tunnel, red and white spotted toadstools to hop on, and a honeycomb structure to climb. There was also a clear pipe with leaf cutter ants that wrapped around the walls. It really was a neat area—but one with plenty of blind spots.

I found a place to set our stuff down and took a seat, making sure all my children knew where to find me. When my kids are in an area like this, I usually explain that they are not allowed to leave the building. They swing by often for snacks, a drink, or to talk to me about something they did or saw. If I haven't seen a particular child in a while, I usually ask another child if they have seen them. If no one has seen them, I get up and wander the area, making sure everyone is accounted for and safe.

On this sunny summer day, my friend was nursing her baby while sitting next to me on the bench and we were chatting about all sorts of mom things. The topic of losing children came up, and we discussed the times we had lost our children. She confessed about the time her two-year-old wandered away at a friend's house with more than twenty acres of land. I had just finished retelling the story about Xander getting lost at the zoo when we both realized our two youngest children were no longer around.

We were not too panicked at first, instead laughing about how we were just talking about losing our children and now our two three-year-olds were lost. We called our older kids over and asked them to spread out, forming a child-led search party. The more eyes, the better.

At least they were together, right? Safety in numbers. But how safe can two three-year-olds really be? That's like a two-for-one deal for a child predator. We called for them, but it soon became obvious they were no longer in the building. They were gone!

Not far from the indoor children's area was a small playground. Parents were milling about, watching their children climb the rock wall and play in the stream. I heard the loud wail of a child who had just fallen and scraped his knee, and the laughter of a group of older children chasing each other. The other parents seemed to be doing their job, watching their children and being responsible. Here I was, frantically wondering where my little girl could be. My friend's oldest son ran up behind me, out of breath. "We found them!" he said. "They're together and inside."

Relief flooded me. Thank God! How many times must I lose a child? If I don't get my shit together, one day I may not be so lucky.

These two little partners in crime had decided it would be a great idea to leave the building and play at the playground together. I'm not sure whose idea it was, her child or mine, but it really doesn't matter. All that matters is that they were found.

My friend and I will never forget the day we sat around discussing losing our children while we LOST our children! Oh, the irony!

I'm not perfect, I make mistakes. Thankfully, these times that I lost my children or left one in a car did not end in tragedy. I thank my lucky stars each day, because not all parents have been this lucky. One small mistake, the blink of an eye, one lapse in judgment has changed the lives of other parents, and my heart breaks for them.

ROCK-BOTTOM MAMA (INTRODUCTION)

I was sitting outside the library one summer day in 2018, waiting to pick up my twelve-year-old. She had been working as a Volunteer for the library's summer reading club. I had fifteen minutes before she was done with her shift. I'd already browsed the library earlier that day and filled my red library bag to the brim with books, so I had no need to go inside. I had no other kids with me—they had stayed home, playing in the woods on our property, while my husband fiddled around in the garage. I decided to use this rare quiet moment to catch up with a friend.

My book came up, and she did not seem thrilled when I told her it was about parenting. She thinks I'm a pretty perfect parent. I'm not, and I tell her this often. I yell, I lose my patience, I sometimes drink wine at 11 a.m., and I lose my children!

I explained that I was writing a book about being an imperfect parent, about how deeply flawed and fucked up I really am. I was giving her some examples of my big mistakes when she audibly sighed, took a long pause, and then opened up to me about her very worst moment in parenting.

She was having a rough year. Her sister had recently committed suicide, and her husband had died suddenly in a car crash. Her marriage wasn't a happy one—there was some really tough stuff going on in her relationship—but that did not make the sudden loss of the father of her children any less devastating. I called often to check on her, and she always said she was doing okay. She was too ashamed to admit what was really going on. I had no idea how bad things were until that day in the car when she told me her worst parenting moment, the moment she calls her "rock bottom." Here is her story, told from her point of view.

ROCK BOTTOM MAMA

It was just months after my husband's death, and I was still deep in depression. I didn't shower. Instead, I stayed in my sweatpants and T-shirt for days. I would wake up in the morning, put dry cereal out for the children to eat, then collapse onto the couch in a haze. I would doze, taking comfort in the ambient noise of Minecraft on the iPad. Toys would clatter and crash, kids would climb on me and drive toy cars up and down my legs, and the hum of high-pitched kids' characters playing on the TV echoed in the distance. The noise let me know I was alive, and my kids were safe.

My kids were young then, ages four, five, and eight years old. My oldest pretty much held things together. I think she liked playing mom, or maybe that's just what I tell myself so I can feel better about the way things were. I didn't confide in any of my friends—no one knew how bad things had gotten. There is such a stigma around depression. I just wanted to be alone so I could wallow in my grief. When a friend did stop by unannounced, I would explain that I was just cleaning, despite my house looking like a wreck! It's okay to look like a hot mess mid-day if you are scrubbing a toilet or deep cleaning the fridge.

It was a Thursday afternoon, and I was dozing on the couch, telling myself that familiar lie, "Tomorrow I'll get up and shower. Tomorrow I will get my shit together. Tomorrow I will re-join society." I had no idea that those words were so true, and that tomorrow was in fact going to be a new day. A new start.

My eyes fluttered open to the sound of nothing. Funny how silence can wake you up. The TV was not playing, there was no chatter of children, it was silent…and silence is never good in a house full of children. I jumped off the couch, tossing the beige cable-knit blanket onto the floor. I looked around for my children. My oldest was alone in her room, playing with a jewelry-making kit.

"Where are your brothers?" I snapped.

"I don't know…playing somewhere!" she responded, irritated at the interruption.

I walked down the hall and saw my front door ajar. I raced outside to peer around, hoping to see my children playing in the front yard. They weren't there. I started running down the street barefoot, in bleach-stained sweats, looking like an unwashed recluse.

We live in an upscale suburban neighborhood with long, twisty roads lined with mature weeping willows. Before my husband died, I would walk with the kids down these familiar streets almost nightly, just as the sun was going down. It was maybe my favorite memory of him. That day, I was in a frantic dash, running from street to street and shouting out my kids' names. I was just about to run back to the house and call 911 when my neighbor pulled up.

"You lookin' for your kids?" he asked, peering through the window of his black Hummer H2.

"Yes. Have you seen them?" I stammer.

"They're a couple streets up, near the main road. Hop in, I'll drive ya there."

As I climbed into the front seat of his meticulously clean vehicle, I felt deeply ashamed. I gazed down at my dirty feet—my big toe was bleeding, probably from stumbling over a rock a few blocks back.

When we got there, I was shocked to find our dog, who habitually runs away, glued to the kids' side like a well-trained canine. Not the misbehaving hound I know well. I leapt from the car, ran over, and pulled them to me with such force I may have given them whiplash.

"What were you doing? Why did you leave the house?"

"We wanted to take a walk and didn't want to bother you. We're sick of being stuck at home all day. I wanna go to the park," my son whined.

We walked back slowly as I held onto our dog's red collar. My two children walked in front of me. I stared at them, in awe of the blessings I had in my life and how I could've lost them all. It was that moment that snapped me out of my funk. How easy it would've been for my children to be snatched right off the street, never to be seen again.

I lost my husband, but my kids lost their father, and I had essentially checked out on them every day as I laid in my coffin of a couch wallowing in my sadness. I was still sad, but I learned to cope with it in healthier ways and to be present for my kids.

*****

My friend had never told me about this event before that day, nor did she ever let on that she was struggling. The only reason she shared this with me was because I explained I was writing a book about parenting mistakes. She feared my judgment and kept all the pain she was in hidden away.

I would not have seen her as weak, I would have seen her as strong, because coming forward and asking for help is a very strong thing to do. I am so proud of her for getting the help she needed after she hit rock bottom. Currently she is remarried, with a thriving business and a new baby.

BABY THIEF

I'm going to take you way back to the year 2001. I was twenty-four, and Sebastian was just a few months old. We were living on the top floor of a three-story apartment complex. Our apartment had a small balcony in the living room with a beautiful view of a four-lane road. Despite the lack of nature, I loved sitting out there and watching cars speed by. My favorite views were always the winter nights at dusk just as the snow was falling. The setting sun created a breathtaking, hazy glow highlighted by pink, amber, and crimson.

One night, I was staring through the window and rocking Sebastian, who was dressed in my favorite cozy royal blue fleece sleeper with a small yellow dinosaur patch on the right side of his chest. We were both happy and content; life was good. I was again reminded that he was my miracle baby, the baby we were told we could never conceive. I was recounting my blessings during this blissful moment when I heard the phone ring.

My mom was calling to catch up and see how her first and only grandson was doing. We chatted for a bit while I sat on the floor playing with Sebastian. After our conversation ended, I placed the phone on the futon couch next to me. Then I headed to the bathroom, leaving my son lying on the floor quietly chewing on a terry cloth pastel frog.

I came out of the bathroom a few minutes later, walked down the short hallway to the living room, and Sebastian was gone!

My four-month-old baby was gone…stolen!

My heart hammering in my chest, I ran to the sliding glass doors and tugged. They were locked, and even if they were unlocked, who was going to scale the side of the building to get up here and steal my baby? Certainly not Spider-Man—he saves people. Stealing babies is not his thing!

I ran to the front door, the only other door in the house, and it was also locked. I looked in the living room again, but he still wasn't there. I had to think. He was just a baby. He couldn't move on his own. He couldn't walk or do anything but lay there. Okay, I got it…someone must have broken in, taken him, and locked the door on the way out.

I knew that didn't make sense, but I ran to my purse anyway to look for my keys. Maybe the landlord came in while I was in the bathroom, took my child, and left. He had keys. No, that didn't make sense. Again, I ran back into the living room, but he still wasn't there.

Maybe I was being really scatterbrained. Maybe I had placed him in his crib or another room? I was rather sleep-deprived and felt like I was in a fog most days. I looked in every room...he wasn't there.

He was gone!

I was panicking, trying to figure out what had happened to my baby while I was in the bathroom for five minutes. There was no rational explanation.

Then I heard a gurgle and coo. I dropped to my hands and knees, looking low, and there he was! My baby, who had not yet learned the magical art of locomotion, was under the futon. He was joyously happy, staring up and touching the black metal bars that supported the cushion.

My baby had rolled over!

He had somehow figured out how to roll over while I was in the bathroom...and I missed it. Oh, that clever little baby, making mommy think she had lost her ever-loving mind!

I pulled him out slowly by his feet. I placed him in the middle of the living room, put a toy just out of his reach, and watched him roll toward it like a champ. I'd never seen him do this before. Perhaps he had been practicing in his crib. I kept repeating this activity, putting the toy just far enough away to make him reach... and he rolled! My baby could roll, and what a trickster he was! What an irrational thought I just had. A baby thief who can scale walls like Spider-Man and magically lock doors as they exit.

I called Joe and excitedly retold the entire story. We had a good laugh about all the silly thoughts that ran through my head. Spider-Man!

THAT'S NOT MY KID

I am not 100 percent sure when this actually happened. I was told this story in 2013 by a good friend of the mom involved in this missing-kid case. I later confirmed it was all true. I'm going to tell it from her perspective.

I was at a children's museum not too far from our house with a few friends and their children. We're all close, our children know each other, and I trust the moms. It was just after 11:30 a.m. when we entered the weird science area of the museum. There are many hands-on activities for kids there, and they were running around having a great time. My friends and I were sitting at the edge of the exhibit on benches, keeping an eye on our children while we chatted. This was when we were approached by a museum worker in a bright yellow shirt.

"Are any of you missing a child?" she asked.

We all looked around. One of my friends stood up to get a better look, scanning the room.

"No, we have all our children," we said.

Thirty minutes went by before the worker came back.

"Are you sure you're not missing a child, a black-haired little girl?" she asked.

We looked around again.

"Nope, we have all our children," I replied.

I kind of chuckled as she walked away...who wouldn't realize their child was missing by now? It had been over an hour. Another fifteen minutes passed, and the kids were asking for food, so we decided it was time to head down to the cafeteria. We gathered our children and were grabbing our strollers, purses, and diaper bags when I realized that Ava was missing.

My dear sweet Ava, my little girl with the dark brown—NOT black—hair. When the woman said a little girl with *black* hair was missing, it had never even occurred to me that she could be referring to one of *my* children. My children all have brown hair varying in shades from medium brown to light brown, certainly not black.

"Has anyone seen Ava?" I asked, but I already knew the answer. I now had to walk up to the front desk and let the snarky woman know that, despite the fact that she had asked us not once but *twice* if we were missing a child, I was indeed missing a child.

I approached the front desk and saw my dear sweet Ava in her blue dress sitting at the counter with another worker. She seemed as happy as she could be, putting together a dinosaur puzzle with an older silver-haired woman whose hair was pulled up in a tight bun and had bright pink glasses resting near the edge of her nose.

"Mommy!" Ava exclaimed, jumping up and waving as she stepped over a juice box and bag of animal crackers they must have given her. "I was missing you...where'd you go? I got to play up here in the special place where kids are not allowed. I got a snack, and they even let me stamp hands and be a real worker like them."

Ava wasn't distressed at all. In fact, she looked calm and was loving all the attention. I couldn't decide if I was happy because she wasn't upset by the fact that her mom had just carelessly lost her, or if I was upset that she wasn't at all bothered.

I thanked the workers for watching over her and apologized for any inconvenience. I walked down to the cafeteria with my social butterfly skipping and humming happily. Ava sat down at the table and told her friends about all her adventures as I passed out our lunches. Once everyone was eating, I asked my friend if she could watch my kids while I ran to the bathroom.

As soon as I made it through the door, I burst into tears, sobbing with passion and excess. It was the shaky, snotty, ugly cry of total desperation. My breakdown lasted five minutes before I splashed some cold water on my face, pulled myself together, and headed back to the table. How on earth did I not notice the fact that *my* child was missing? Especially after I was asked not once, but *twice?*

When I was told this story, my heart went out to this mama. What an emotional ordeal to go through. Lucky for her and her child this turned out okay.

OF ALL PLACES, WALMART

Walmart has a stigma—have you seen the videos called "The People of Walmart"? They feature trashy employees and customers that are half-dressed or in pajamas while walking through the store. I'm not sure what started this...maybe lower prices bring in lower-class people? I shop there, and I don't go to the store in pajamas, nor am I lower-class. But I was especially embarrassed about losing my child in a Walmart, because in my head that is something that a lower-class person would do. But would they? Mistakes don't discriminate, no matter our race, class, or gender.

I headed off to Walmart because they have the cheapest cat food—and having eleven barn cats means we go through a lot of food. They do a great job of hunting rodents, but we always keep dry food in the barn in case they would rather fill up on that instead of mouse meat!

Harvard did a study a while back, putting night cameras on domesticated indoor cats to see what they'd do if they were left outside all night. Guess what they found out? Cats will hunt relentlessly all night long, not for food but for sport. They are adorable killing machines!

Last year, when my daughter Alexis decided to camp outside in the woods with a friend, the barn cats were excited to have new visitors. In appreciation of the company, a few of the cats brought over freshly hunted voles and dropped them at their feet while they roasted marshmallows in front of the campfire. Roasted vole, anyone? I'm always sad to see the cute dead rodents, but that's why we have barn cats—they have a purpose, and they're very well loved in return.

So, back to Walmart. I was with my four younger children. My youngest at the time, Bailey, was just three years old. As we walked through the glass double doors, one of the younger boys stated he needed new shoes. I sometimes buy shoes from Walmart because my boys are so hard on shoes that even if I buy expensive, higher-quality shoes, they wear out just as fast. So I buy the cheap ones. Xander was trying on shoes, while Bailey was walking up and down the aisle looking at shoes and singing to herself. My other children were busy annoying each other for entertainment as they waited not-so-patiently nearby.

After a few pairs, Xander found ones that fit and he liked them well enough, given his lack of choices. I placed them in the cart and noticed Bailey was gone.

"Have you guys seen Bailey?" I asked.

They all shrugged. "Nope."

"She was just right here two seconds ago," said my oldest daughter, who was eleven.

I quickly walked up and down the four shoe aisles. She wasn't there!

"Spread out and look for Bailey!" I shouted to my kids.

After a quick search, I realized she wasn't close by—she could be clear on the other side of the store, or in an unmarked van on her way to a ramshackle house with a soiled, stained mattress on the basement floor inside a rusty cage with a lone lightbulb swinging above.

I panicked.

"Xander, Tyler, stay together and go find the toy section and look for Bailey. Do not leave the store with anyone and stay together," I said, wondering if my imaginary shady guy in his unmarked van wanted to scoop the rest of my kids up too!

I raced to the opposite side of the store, past the children's clothing, calling out her name and looking under clothing racks. I reached the frozen food section, and still no sign of her. I sent my oldest daughter to the front of the store to look for her when I spotted a blue-vested Walmart employee stocking frozen pizzas.

Trying to catch my breath and speak in coherent sentences, I said, "My daughter is missing. She's three and was last seen in the shoe section. I turned around, and she was gone!"

He said something into his walkie talkie that I didn't pay attention to, as I was facing the other direction, scanning and listening intently for her voice.

"What does she look like and what was she wearing?" he asked.

"She has long, dark, curly hair and is wearing a pink coat." That was all I could remember about her clothing. Why on earth could I not recall what I dressed her in? It may have been the most important information I needed to remember all day.

Two more employees joined us. "We have all employees on alert, and they have people stationed at the front doors looking for any child who comes close to her description."

I walked back toward the shoe section, passing the toddler's and kids' clothing and calling her name.

Ahead, a slender, dark-haired woman wearing a pink and blue plaid shirt was staring at me, motioning for me to look down the shoe aisle. I scanned the aisle, but I didn't see anything significant. She moved closer and whispered, "I heard the missing child announcement and found her a few minutes later when I was looking for slippers. I just stood here, keeping an eye on her a safe distance away. I didn't want to touch her or talk to her for fear that someone would think I was a kidnapper and tackle me. My little brother does this to us all the time."

I looked down the aisle and saw Bailey curled under a metal bench. It was just big enough for a small child to fit underneath. Relief flooded my body.

She is safe, she is here.

I pulled her little body into my arms and squeezed her tight.

"You found me, Mommy. Now you hide, and I go find you!"

She thought we were playing a game! Here I was in a state of panic, thinking someone stole my child and had her tied up in the back of an unmarked white van, heading far out of town, while she was gleefully playing a game of hide-and-go-seek, silent as a mouse.

I thanked the woman in the plaid shirt, then grabbed the closest Walmart employee to thank him and let him know my child had been found.

The day before, my younger boys—ages eight and nine—had taught Bailey how to play hide-and-go-seek. She was unaware this was an unacceptable game to play in a public place, nor a game you should start without telling everyone else that the game had begun.

SAFE AND SOUND

Thankfully, every one of these instances had a happy ending. Occasionally there is a horrific story about a child abduction that makes us hold tight to the ones we hold dear, but after a quick Google search those are few and far between. There are about

500,000 missing children each year. Of those missing children, about 1,400 are kidnappings done by a family member. Only about 150 each year are done by a stranger, and those usually occur within a quarter-mile of their homes. Out of the 150 stranger abductions, 90 percent come home safely, so that leaves about fifteen kids a year who are taken away, never to be seen again.

Have a talk with your kids. Tell them about stranger danger and what they should do if they find themselves lost. The odds are in your favor, mamas. Of all the missing children cases, most return home safely. So relax a little and try not to panic too much if you find your child missing.

Pro tip: Take a photo of your children when you arrive at an amusement park or busy place where they may get lost. This way, you have a current picture of your children and don't have to remember what they're wearing that day. In this age of cell phone usage, you can quickly spread this photo to emergency workers and find your missing child faster than ever before.

CHAPTER 8

My New Body— The Mom Bod

Did you ever see *those* pregnant moms? You know, the gorgeous and glowing ones who are super fit and who worked out through their entire pregnancies and have the cutest little basketball bellies? I am friends with a few of those moms, and my hat goes off to them. However, that was not me. I looked like a refrigerator through all but one of my pregnancies—the very last one, when I was thirty-six years old. I'm going to get very personal in this chapter, so grab a glass of wine and dig in...or just skip this chapter and move on. The choice is yours. But don't say I didn't warn you!

I've heard before that it takes nine months to grow your baby, so it should take at least nine months to get your body back. This seems logical, but it's definitely not a one-size-fits-all theory. I gained eighty whopping pounds with my first and between twenty and fifty pounds with my four other babies. I did get back to my pre-pregnancy weight after Sebastian, but my body shape had changed into my new "mom body." This was a hard pill to swallow at first—how could I weigh the same and still not fit into my pants?

The answer is simple: my body morphed into my new mama bear state.

Have you ever watched a time-lapse video showing how a woman's organs compress and move out of the way to make room for baby? If you haven't, I suggest you do a quick Google search and watch one. It's amazing to watch the organs smoosh down and move out of the way to make room for a growing baby. Did you also know that your abdominal muscles actually separate? Pretty darn amazing, if you ask me, and no wonder our bodies may not look the same after children.

It's hard to not feel down about yourself when you see post-baby images of celebrities on social media platforms. They look great, and kudos to them, but this is not how most moms look. Celebrities need to look good—their job depends on it. Can you imagine how stressful that must be, knowing that if you don't get back in shape fast, you may not get that next movie deal to pay for your giant house? To know that people are watching you and snapping pictures of you looking like a hot mess when you're buying diapers at the store?

Let's stop comparing ourselves to others and focus on being the best we can be. The grass always looks greener on the other side. We all have our own battles and obstacles, let's support each other. We are all on our own journey.

I AM FIERCE—HEAR ME ROAR

I gained a lot of weight with all my children, and I worked my ass off after baby number one to get my body back. Although my shape mostly returned, carrying and giving birth to an almost ten-pound baby took its toll. I was left with plenty of stretch marks. Strangely, none of these stretch marks ended up on my belly. I had hundreds of bright pink striations on my thighs and breasts. The front of my thighs looked as if they were shredded by the relentless claws of a fierce beast—they were my battle scars. But *I am* that fierce beast. Motherhood turned me into a warrior. As

Motherhood
TURNED ME INTO A
warrior.
AS MY CHILD CHANGED
AND GREW INSIDE ME,
I changed as well;
A FIERCE MAMA BEAR
WAS FORMING INSIDE
ME, RIGHT ALONGSIDE
MY INFANT.

my child changed and grew inside me, I changed as well; a fierce mama bear was forming inside me, right alongside my infant.

In time, I came to love my stretch marks as a physical representation of the changes that happened to me as I became a mother. The marks eventually faded to a lighter pink, then to a shade slightly lighter than my actual skin color. They're still there...never erased, never gone. At first, I was very self-conscious of these markings, not because they were there but because they were on my thighs. Most moms I knew had them across their bellies. It wasn't the stretch marks themselves that were making me feel self-conscious, it was the strange placement. It wasn't until baby number five, my last child, that I spotted one single stretch mark near my belly button. I found this rather comical, since my last baby was not my largest and this pregnancy was my fittest one. I had only gained twenty pounds and was sixty pounds lighter than I had been for the previous four babies.

When I had my first baby, I was still twenty-three, so my physical appearance meant a lot to me. My job also depended on it, but that story is for another book, another time. After my second baby, I didn't bounce back. I then proceeded to have multiple babies back to back, never fully getting back to my pre-baby size between pregnancies. My weight has bounced all around over the last twenty years. My highest weight was 215 lbs. on the day I birthed my first child and my lowest was 125 lbs.

I have worked out consistently over the years, always trying to set a good example for my children and stressing the importance of a healthy lifestyle and cardiovascular activity. It's not how you look, but how you feel.

The thing that keeps me going, even if I cannot see a physical change in my body, is knowing that my stamina gets better with each workout. If I ever needed to physically run from danger, could I do that? How long could I keep it up? How far could I go? Could I do it while carrying a child? This is what keeps me going. I am their mama bear, their fierce protector.

I need to be strong for them; I need to at least be fit enough that I could save them. I also need to make sure I treat my body well so I can watch them flourish and have their own babies some-day. I am determined to live to one hundred—and not just any one hundred, but a healthy hundred!

I keep that thought in my head when I work out. It's what gets me moving on the days I don't want to move. It keeps me running five more minutes when it's getting hard and I want to quit.

When I was young, I worked out to look good. Now, at age forty-two, I work out to live a long, healthy life.

Motherhood changes our bodies, and it's different for every mom. You may be rounder and carry weight in places you never did before. You may weigh the same as you did before, but with a different body shape. Before children, I had a perfect hourglass shape—my friends coveted my body. After children, my breasts shrank, my waistline grew, and my hips filled out to a much rounder size. It's okay. I don't mind. In fact, I actually like my rounder hips. The rest…well, not so much, but it's a work in prog-ress and a small price to pay for five beautiful children.

CAN YOU COME IN THE BATHROOM AND LOOK AT THIS?

Stress incontinence is something all women talk about—there's not one female I'm friends with who doesn't have this issue to some degree. My mother had a serious case of incontinence after she had children. If she had a full bladder and coughed, sneezed, or laughed, she would pee her pants and completely soak herself. She told me kids did this to her, so I was always terrified that if I had children it would happen to me as well. Luckily, I haven't had this issue. I did, however, develop my own issues from birthing five large babies.

One day, I was standing at the kitchen sink washing dishes when I had the sensation of a tampon sliding out of me. This was strange because I was not on my period. I dried my hands and walked to the bathroom to check out what was going on. When I pulled my pants down and looked between my legs, I was horrified. A firm, golf-ball-sized piece of my body was protruding out of my birth canal. It was most certainly attached to me and definitely not something that should be hanging out.

Cancer! Oh God, I have a large tumor!

"Joe!" I yelled. "I need you to come here...NOW!"

Joe approached the bathroom door carefully. "What?" he asked, standing outside the door.

"I need you to come in here and look at something," I whisper.

"What is it?" he said, clearly irritated.

"There's something falling out of me that clearly shouldn't be. I can't see it very well, so I need you to look and tell me what you see."

"I'm not going to know what I'm looking at."

"Well, dear," I said, "you've put your face in that area for the last fifteen years. That makes you extremely qualified to know what normal and abnormal looks like!"

He sighed heavily and pushed into the room. "FINE."

I positioned myself on the edge of the tub and spread my legs so he could see.

"You should have that looked at by a doctor," he said, barely looking.

"Well, what does it look like exactly? Is it a tumor? What color is it? Describe it!" I said, fuming at his lack of effort.

When he didn't answer, I said, "You know what, just go get my phone. I'll take a picture of it."

I could not believe what a baby he was being—I was the one with the problem. Part of my body was falling out of me, and my husband couldn't be bothered to help me figure out what it was.

I took a few pictures, in case a medical professional wanted to see it, then I shoved my lady bits back up inside me where they belonged.

I called my midwife's emergency number, left a message, and waited for the phone to ring while I paced in our bedroom. I was infuriated by my husband's lack of help and panicked by what could be happening. The phone rang a few minutes later. I spoke in detail about the situation to the midwife. I also let her know I had pictures if she needed them, but she didn't want them. She was confident that my uterus had prolapsed. This is normal for many women, especially after birthing five large babies. She told me to come into the office on Monday. In the meantime, she told me to wear tight underwear and keep my legs closed for the rest of the weekend.

I certainly wasn't going to open my legs for my husband after how he had just acted!

Two days later, I was sitting half naked on crinkly paper covering a beige table, wearing a pink and white gown with my ass hanging out the back. The midwife gave me a thorough examination where I had to stand with my legs spread while she laid on the floor and looked up with a flashlight at my girl parts while asking me to bear down.

Mortifying.

She concluded that my bladder, rectum, and uterus were all prolapsed. She explained that my options included surgery if I chose to stop having children, and that if I did choose to have more children, it would get worse and possibly lead to further complications.

Worse? Oh God, I cannot do worse. I already had to stuff my organs back into my body multiple times over the weekend.

I decided against surgery and was heartbroken that another child was not in the cards. I wanted Bailey, my youngest, to have a sibling close in age. I would no longer be able to provide that for her.

My body made that choice for me, and I was mad! But I reminded myself of how blessed I really was—I already had five healthy babies. This was amazing, because I'd been told it would be unusual if I had one, let alone five. As sad as it was for me to know that my baby days were over, it was really a blessing. My oldest was fifteen when I found this out. It really opened my eyes to the moments happening right in front of me. So much of Sebastian's upbringing was a blur because I was so exhausted.

Since I found this out, I've been more present and engaged with my children than ever before. The years go so fast.

Sebastian had me all to himself for five years before I introduced another child. He still remembers those days—he was my world, my miracle, and I savored every moment. My middle kids got the shorter end of the stick—they had to share me with their siblings, and it was hard to really savor every moment when I was so tired. My last child gets more attention because now I know just how quickly it goes. Sebastian, now nineteen, lives in his own house with his girlfriend, who I adore. He's no longer in my house, no longer under my protective wing. I was sad to see him go, but so proud he was ready to start his life and make his own mark on the world.

The year after my diagnosis was hard. I couldn't work out like I wanted because every time I squatted, I had to shove my uterus back inside me. I went to physical therapy, but they just wanted me to do Kegels, and that wouldn't help. They're not even the same muscles. After searching online groups, I came across the book *Diastasis Recti, The Whole-Body Solution to Abdominal Weakness and Separation* by Katy Bowman. This book was a life-changer. She discusses issues like abdominal separations, hernias, and prolapsed organs caused by trauma and weakness in the midsection of a woman's body from childbirth.

She wrote about simple things, like the way I was standing with my back more arched, to supporting a belly full of baby or holding a baby after birth. Subtle changes in the way we stand, sit, and hold our babies may cause weakness in certain muscles. Her book helped me really understand what was wrong, all the muscles that were affected, and how to fix it.

Along with this book, I started an exercise program called MuTu, which focuses on slowly healing damaged muscles. Six months later, I had lost twenty pounds and was feeling better and fit again. I continued this program for over a year and slowly started incorporating the exercises that had once caused my organs to fall out.

Today, I am fit and strong. I exercise four to six days a week, although I'm still limited on which exercises I can do because of my weak pelvic floor. I have learned to work around these issues, and when needed I just stuff my organs back inside and move on with my day.

TINKLE, TINKLE LITTLE...BLADDER!

An unfortunate side effect of having my organs prolapse is that sometimes it causes me to use the bathroom urgently and frequently. I pee more now than I did when I was pregnant; sometimes I may only go a little bit, but still feel as if my bladder is going to explode. When this happens, it's usually caused by my uterus pushing forward and pressing down on my bladder, like being pregnant and having a baby pushing there.

A few weeks ago, my oldest needed a ride to class because his car wouldn't start. I had somewhere to be, so after I finished my fourth cup of coffee, I jumped in the car to race him off to class, still hoping to make it to the doctor's appointment I had on the other side of town. I usually pee before I leave the house, but I was in a hurry, so I didn't. About halfway to school, I realized I needed to pee—four cups of coffee and an unpredictable bladder can cause a wee bit of insecurity.

I can make it.

I dropped him off at school but *really* needed to pee. I wriggled around in my seat like a four-year-old.

I can make it, the drive is only twenty minutes.

I pulled into the medical complex parking lot. The bathroom was on the opposite side of the building from my doctor's office, so I pulled around to the back of the building, closer to the bathrooms. I got out of the car, and as I stood up the gravity set in—the weight pushing down on my bladder was almost crippling.

Oh no! I really need to pee.

I walked to the door...it was locked!

> ## Office Staff Only
> ## Please Use the West Doors

Oh no!

I started the very long walk to the open door on the far side of the building. It was a seven-minute walk. I didn't think I had seven minutes. I stood there for a minute, legs crossed and trying to figure out what to do.

I may actually pee my pants.

Walking wasn't going to work. If I drove to the front of the building and parked near the main doors, I'd be closer to the bathroom. So I got back into the car, thinking maybe I should just park near the back of the lot and pee in the empty Starbucks cup from yesterday. I looked around in my van, but it was gone.

Dammit!

I had cleaned out the trash from my car the day before and threw it away.

I seriously might pee my pants.

I parked as near the entrance as I could, which was still a decent walk to the bathroom.

I can do this. I am a grown-ass woman, I cannot pee my pants.

I got out of the car again—this time I almost peed my pants the moment I stood up. I stood with legs crossed, just staring at the ground. My hands started shaking, my heart racing.

I am not going to make it.

I started to run, but quickly stopped as the sudden up-and-down motion was sure to cause me to spring a leak. I walked very slowly to the entrance with my legs as crossed as I could get them and still walk. I looked rather silly with my crossed-legged prance, like a seven-year-old fashionista trying to walk down the runway with a very exaggerated hip sway. I slowly placed one foot in front of the other. I had to stop every five feet to tightly cross my legs. I pulled my phone from my pocket to stare at while I was stopped, pretending to read a text so I wouldn't look like a complete weirdo. I was near tears. I was so overcome with emotion at the prospect of wetting myself. I was also mad at myself. Was I really a five-year-old who waited too long to go potty? Yeah, pretty much.

I'm not going to make it.

During one of my dramatic pauses, I wondered if my body decided to let go, would it be a noticeable gush? Would my pants absorb most of it? Would people notice? Would there be a puddle? There were people all around me. If I did pee my pants, should I go to the doctor anyway, soaked in my own urine, or just go home and cry?

I made it to the glass doors. An older gentleman held the door open, so I was forced to walk a little faster than I wanted to in an effort to not be rude.

This is it...I am going to pee!

But I didn't. I made it past the doors and saw the blue sign with the white stick figure in a dress. The ladies' room. It's right there. So close. I made it inside.

I am gonna make it!

Like the Little Engine that Could.

I threw open the stall door and dropped my purse haphazardly, causing the contents to spill everywhere. I didn't even bother shutting the stall door as I did the wiggle dance small children do and fumbled with the button on my jeans.

Why did I choose jeans? Yoga pants would've been easier.

I shimmied down my red Victoria's Secret panties and released the floodgates as I slowly pushed shut the stall door with my left hand. I may have peed the most I ever have in my life; I didn't think I was ever going to stop.

I made it!

I should have known better—I'm not three years old! I'm in my forties, with an unstable bladder from the complications of birthing five children. Never again will I wait that long, because next time, I just may not make it!

LET IT FLOW

Sure, I have dribbled a little here and there, during a sneeze, cough, or deep squat at the gym, but I have birthed five children and it just comes with the territory. Of all the moms I know, there's not one mom who hasn't had some sort of bladder leakage, either during pregnancy or afterward. Just recently a friend told me that every time she did a pull-up at the gym, she peed a little.

Meredith from "That's Inappropriate" shared on her Instagram story today that she "peed in her pantaloons" as she was waiting to get off her flight in Louisville, Kentucky, after a Delta flight attendant refused her access to the bathroom after the landing gear had come down.

Carrying a baby really takes a toll on your body. I am still amazed by the sheer magnificence of a woman's body. We grow life, then produce the food to sustain these small wonders. Women are beautiful, no matter their shape and size. Women everywhere should wear their mom bodies proudly because that body underwent the most amazing process ever known to humankind. So stand up tall and be proud of these changes, even if that means wearing waterproof underwear!

THE WAVY BUTT

"Are all butts wavy like yours?" my thirteen-year-old son asked as I was walking through the house in my underwear and T-shirt, trying to locate a pair of clean pants.

Yikes, it's not like I didn't already know my butt and the backs of my legs were covered in cellulite. I had always battled cellulite, even when I was a very fit eighteen-year-old. Not much, but it was there, as I grew and shrank multiple times over the years. Whether I was a size four or a size twelve, cellulite was there like an uninvited guest, refusing to leave.

"No, not all people have cellulite," I responded.

After I finished getting dressed, I pulled up some information on cellulite so he could better understand why it's there. I'm a research junkie and am always looking stuff up, especially if it's a question my kids ask. I want to be able to give my children accurate facts and show them that if I don't know the answer, I can find it. Knowing how to get answers is one of the most empowering tools you can give your children. Lead by example, even if your butt is wavy!

Women everywhere SHOULD WEAR THEIR MOM BODIES *proudly* BECAUSE THAT BODY UNDERWENT THE MOST *amazing process ever known to humankind.*

SLIP AND SLIDE: WHEN YOU UNDERESTIMATE YOUR AGE

Growing up in the 1980s, plastic slip and slides were all the rage, although they have been around since Wham-O introduced them in 1961. I would spend hours outside, running from across the neighbor's yard to jump onto the plastic sheet and slide down on my belly. We came up with all sorts of combinations to accelerate faster. We tried baby oil, Crisco, and different types of soap. Every kid in the neighborhood came over, and sometimes the line was twelve kids deep. Remember, this was the 1980s, before cable and smartphones, so everyone was outside. Moms would stop by with extra popsicles and hang out in the front yard, sitting on multicolored woven lawn chairs, smoking cigarettes, and doing whatever moms in the 1980s did without smartphones.

Those hot summers were loaded with fun. Our stomachs would be bright red from friction and grass burns, but we didn't feel it—we were young, invincible, and living our best lives.

When Sebastian was about four years old, I saw a slip and slide on the shelf of a Toys 'R Us. Naturally, I grabbed it and placed it in the cart, hoping to give my own child the joy I once had from this amazing invention.

We waited for a hot enough summer day to withstand the frigid hose water. I'm sure he wouldn't have minded, but I wanted to play too, and I was not ready to endure cold hose water unless it was a really hot day. I got it all set up, hammered down the plastic pegs to hold it in place, and turned the hose on. I backed up to get a head start and took off running toward the long yellow plastic runway. I launched my twenty-seven-year-old body toward the ground and landed with a SMACK! I felt like I'd been dropped from an airplane. The ground felt as hard as concrete and I only slid about three feet. I slowly got up, hurting everywhere, and saw Joe standing in the driveway with his arms crossed, laughing at me.

"Doesn't that look fun?" I said to Sebastian, who was staring wide-eyed at me.

He ran over to the grass and took off like I did, except he didn't fall hard and get stuck midway. He sailed effortlessly to the end with a splash!

"This is fun, Mommy, can I do it again?" he squealed.

"You can do it all day, dear," I said.

I stood there watching him and wondering what I had done wrong. I did it just like he did but, man, it hurt when I landed, and I didn't even slide that far! I was a very fit 125 pounds at the time, so there seemed to be no reason I didn't slide like my son.

Soap!

I needed soap to lube it up and get it nice and slippery. I ran into the house and grabbed the dish soap from the kitchen sink, squirted it liberally on the plastic, then backed up to try again. Joe was staring at me, shaking his head at my stupidity.

I smiled at him, then took off running again. I hit the slide hard again—it still felt like concrete, but with the soap I flew down the slide faster. I was laughing out loud, up until I hit the end and kept going, flipping across the grass in a sideways somersault. Landing face first in the dirt, I was no longer laughing. I slowly got up and assessed my wounds, feeling like a Mack truck had hit me.

"Whoa! That's cool! I wanna try!" Sebastian shouted.

Before I could warn him to go slow, he was already sliding down fast and smooth. But he didn't end up face-first in the grass like me. Instead, he landed safely in the splash pool.

Sebastian played for hours that day. He was soon joined by our water-loving black lab, who kept laying in the middle of the slide and biting at the water, preventing Sebastian from getting to the end. He didn't mind—we laughed and had fun with the dog. I watched Sebastian from my bench swing as I sat sipping an iced tea. Life was good.

Fast forward ten years, four more children, and a farmhouse on fifteen acres. I bought another slip and slide for all five kids to enjoy. I was smart enough this time around to not go down the slip and slide myself. Sebastian only went down a few times, while all the little kids had a blast sliding to the end over and over again. They seemed to enjoy it, but when I mentioned getting another one the following summer, they all said it hurt too much!

THE TALLEST SLEDDING HILL IN NORTHWEST OHIO

I love sledding—it's one of my happiest childhood memories. Both my parents would head out to our favorite sledding spot with my brother and I and zoom down the hill, snow flying up in our faces. My parents would laugh and throw snowballs…it was just a magical experience.

I wanted to recreate this experience with my own children, so every time it snows, we head out to local sledding hills. Joe has come along a few times, but he really hates everything having to do with cold weather. He doesn't even like going down a hill. Who grows up in the Midwest and dislikes flying down a hill at full speed? My husband…that's who! There are actually a lot of people who live in Ohio but hate the cold; I don't get it!

Last summer, while we were on a kayaking trip with our Girl Scout troop, a Metropark employee told us that Blue Creek has the tallest man-made sledding hill in northwest Ohio. I made a mental note to check that out in the winter, and that's exactly what we did.

In January 2019, I scheduled a snowshoeing field trip at Blue Creek for our Scouts. There was just an inch of snow, not nearly enough for snowshoeing, so we ended up doing a geology tour and checking out fossils in the park's quarry and glacier grooves. It's mindboggling to think that the area where we live used to be covered in large glaciers.

I had texted parents earlier that day to bring sleds. There was just a dusting of snow on the hill, with big patches of grass and dirt showing through. The hill looked big, but not huge as we trucked up, using the handy steps. Once I was standing at the top, it looked a bit intimidating. Xander went down first, fast as ever and squealing the whole way.

"This is awesome!" he yelled up when he reached the bottom.

I stood there looking down the hill, a little afraid. If I fell off my sled, I could easily break something. I positioned myself on our orange and green plastic sled (the wooden toboggan I grew up riding was stowed in the garage loft). Before I could fully situate myself, I was already sliding down, fast as ever. I put my feet out to slow my very rough, bumpy, and slightly scary descent.

I laughed out loud the entire trip, reaching the bottom safe and sound at an incredible speed. I got off the sled still smiling, and watched Alexis zoom down and then head right back up the hill for round two.

I climbed back to the top again, marveling at the pink, orange, and blue marbled sky. I positioned myself on my knees this time to help cushion against the bumpy ride down, but then quickly decided against it. So back on my butt I went, and it was much faster this time. The wind whipped past my face, and I felt like a joyous child again.

Then I hit a large bump that sent me airborne, and with little snow to cushion my landing, I came down hard and felt the impact radiate up my spine from my tailbone.

I sat at the bottom for a few minutes before struggling to get up. I had cracked my tailbone once in sixth grade, so I knew exactly how it felt. I slowly walked over to the fence, watching the kids zoom down the hill over and over.

"Are you going down again?" my kids asked.

"Nope, I broke my ass. Quite literally. I'm struggling to walk. You go, have fun. I am just going to watch," I said as they cracked up at my foul language and the fact that my butt was broken.

I should've known better, but I don't want to be that mom who doesn't try things or refuses to participate in the fun. I want to do all the things possible with my kids to make awesome memories. Will I be heading down the hill again? I sure will, but next time I will make sure there is more snow for a nice cushion on my rear end.

CHAPTER 9

When the Smoke Clears

FIRE!

It was Thanksgiving Day, 2012, when I was abruptly awakened at 5:30 a.m. by the shrill sound of a fire alarm going off. I knew immediately it was the dryer. I shook Joe awake and yelled, "Fire... the dryer is on fire!"

I thought some wires had melted, or maybe it had overheated because the mechanism that turns off the dryer when the cycle is over no longer worked. Then I remembered. I had never turned the dryer off after I took the pumpkin pies from the oven the night before.

I raced down to the basement, the smell of smoke increasing as I turned the corner to see bright orange flames erupting from the dryer. Joe pushed past me and quickly pulled the dryer door open. The inside of the dryer was engulfed in flames, and black smoke quickly filled the room. My lungs started protesting, and they burned fiercely with every panicked breath.

"Get some water!" Joe shouted.

I don't know why he wanted water because we have a fire extinguisher, but I just blindly followed his instructions. As much as I like to think I act fast and efficiently in an emergency, I don't. I stood there looking at the flames, frozen in horror. Joe, however, takes the cake on this one. He is the yin to my yang, and can rock an emergency with swift, actionable results. So, I raced upstairs to the kitchen, filled up a bucket, and brought it back down. He doused the fire, but it did nothing to the flames. The fire was the size of a decent campfire, but we weren't happy campers cooking s'mores. This fire could burn our house to the ground if we didn't act fast.

He pointed to the utility sink three feet from the dryer. We never used this sink because it didn't drain properly. He gestured for me to use that water. I hesitated, knowing the sink would get plugged, but then I thought: would a little extra water be a bad thing right now? I suppose not!

"Should I call 911?" I yelled over the shrill of multiple fire alarms echoing through the house.

"No, we got this!" he yelled back.

My lungs were burning so bad it felt like I was inhaling acid. I had never imagined smoke could hurt like that. The room was so smoky I could hardly see. My eyes were watering, but I kept looking at the rafters above the dryer, knowing that was where my daughter's bed was, where she was still sleeping soundly. My gut kept screaming at me to get the kids out and call 911. Joe, meanwhile, was throwing water on the fire, sending billows of smoke into the room. He had covered his face with a towel, so I copied him and grabbed a white shirt from the top of a pile of dirty laundry. It didn't help. With every breath, I wanted to scream in sheer agony.

Joe was still trying to fight the flames, too stubborn to call 911. I dropped the shirt, leaving Joe behind to play firefighter, and headed upstairs to get the kids out of the house and call 911.

"Wake up, wake up! Fire! Fire! There's a fire in the house! We need to get out!" I shouted.

My twelve-year-old son thought it was just a fire drill. He casually strutted down the stairs with a cocky smile spreading across his face. We touch on the subject of fire safety each October, during national fire prevention month, and we had just had a drill in the middle of the night to be better prepared. But tonight, there was an actual fire.

"This is not a drill! There is a real FIRE!" I shouted.

Maybe he heard the fear in my voice, maybe it was the smell of smoke, or possibly he heard the smoke alarms. I don't know which, but he picked up his pace. My two other children were now awake and coming out of their room as well.

"Fire! There's a fire in the basement, go outside!"

Soon all my children were out safely, shivering in the 20-degree weather in just pajamas.

"Stay here, I will be right back!"

I ran back inside—not for valuables or things that have memories, but for the keys to the van so my shivering children could at least stay warm.

Inside, I saw that the main floor was filling with smoke. I grabbed the keys, then ran from room to room, opening windows. The smell was horrific, and I didn't want my entire house to be filled with this noxious odor. I also snatched a few blankets along the way.

Not long after my call to 911, we stood staring at our house in the early morning hours, shivering and wrapped in blankets. All I could do was think about how much I had to be thankful for this year. Yes, our dryer was on fire and there may have been significant damage, but we were all safe and unharmed. Then I remembered Joe. I had left him in the basement just before calling 911. Just then, he came stumbling out of the house, bent over clutching his chest and coughing, no longer playing the part of firefighter Fred.

He was safe—we were all safe.

We could faintly hear the fire trucks, getting louder as they approached. I tried to get the kids to focus on how neat it was.

Eight fire trucks arrived, and they quickly went to work and did their magic. Luckily, the dryer was against a concrete wall and sitting on a concrete floor. The fire captain said that if the dryer had been on anything else but concrete, or next to anything else but concrete, our house would have absolutely gone up in flames.

It was a terrifying thought, because two of my children slept just above where the fire had started. Would I have gotten to my children in time?

The firefighters put out the fire quickly, then hauled the dryer up the stairs to the driveway outside.

"Who opened all the windows?" the fire chief asked.

"Me! That was me...I didn't want the smoke to make the house smell," I replied.

"You realize that oxygen feeds a fire, and that your decision to open the windows could have caused a catastrophic spread of this fire?" the chief said rather cockily.

"Well, yes...I realize that now, but at the time I just wanted that smell to get out of my house, it was so bad. Thankfully you guys got here when you did. Thank you so much for helping us."

*****

Let's back up to a few weeks before the fire.

I had noticed that the dryer was continuing to run long after what I thought was an hour. After some troubleshooting, I realized that the only way to stop the dryer was to open the dryer door or unplug the machine. It no longer stopped at the end of the cycle.

If the dryer door was shut, the dryer automatically turned on. The only way to prevent this was to open the dryer door. If I put a load in the dryer, I had to set a timer to remind myself to open the door or it would run indefinitely. I didn't want to spend the money on fixing it because Christmas was coming soon.

When I had turned the dryer on the night before, I set the timer on the stove for sixty minutes. Unfortunately, I was also putting pumpkin pies in the oven. So, when the timer went off, I pulled the pies out, completely forgetting about the clothing in the dryer. Then I went to bed.

When the fire alarms went off, I knew exactly what it was. How could I have been so careless? How could I have forgotten something so important? My babies could have burnt up because I forgot something so important.

My youngest lost his favorite stuffed giraffe in that fire. He had asked for it before he went to bed that evening, but it was in the dryer. Poor sad Giraffe; he perished in that fire. If only I had remembered.

We were all safe, and our house only suffered about two thousand dollars in damages. How thankful we really were on that Thanksgiving morning.

The following week we baked cookies for the firemen who had saved us. We made cookies in the shapes of people and houses. My oldest said it was fitting because they had saved us and our house. We delivered them the following week, on what they call "tool day," when they test all their tools and make sure everything is in good working order. The firemen were excited to have a captivated audience, and gave us a detailed explanation of all the tools they use to fight fires and all the equipment on the trucks.

I'm not sure why I thought I would remember to turn the dryer off when I seemed to forget the simplest of things. I often wondered if I was losing my mind, but I wasn't. I was just suffering from "mom brain." According to an article in *Psychology Today*, researchers have discovered physical changes that happen to women's brains after they give birth, proving that "mom brain" is real and not just an excuse.

ANOTHER FIRE

During fall 2018 I was cooking bacon in the oven from our newly slaughtered hogs. We raised a special heritage breed prized for their optimal lard, but they also created a lot of grease. In this case, there was about an inch of grease in the pan. Just as I was pulling the baking sheet from the oven, my four-year-old came running around the corner. I jerked the pan back so I wouldn't burn her, spilling hot grease into the oven and causing an instant fire.

POOF!

The oven went immediately up in flames as I yelled for everyone to get outside. I searched for my phone, but I couldn't find it. I came across my daughter's phone, but quickly realized it was password protected. Although she had told me her password, I couldn't recall it. I held her phone while still searching for mine when I remembered her password. I punched it in and dialed 911.

"Nine-one-one, what's your emergency?"

"Hi, I'm having a grease fire, but I cannot remember if I should use water or a fire extinguisher on it. There's weird rules about grease fires."

"I'm not sure," the young male 911 operator said.

"Wait, what? You don't know?" I should have just Googled it. "Don't send help. I'll just look it up, the flames are not that big now."

"Help is on the way, don't worry," he said.

Ugh, I should have just Googled this. The fire was nearly gone by then.

I soon saw fire trucks outside sitting by our gate. I thought they were wondering if they could fit down the drive. We lived on fifteen gated acres in the woods, and you can't see our house from the road. I wondered how much damage my house would have suffered if there had been a legit fire and they sat out there deciding what to do.

I went back inside to check the oven. The fire was out, and I felt like an idiot for calling at all. The fire trucks finally made it up our long, wooded drive, and firefighters barreled out of the truck in full fire gear. I stood on the porch, the kids in the front yard dancing and playing. I let the firefighters know there was no longer a fire as they headed inside, but they ignored me and marched past. When they saw with their own eyes what I had just told them, they ripped off their masks and other fire gear and reported that it was a false alarm. I was feeling like an idiot when the fire chief got out of his SUV and asked if he could come inside and talk to me about what had happened. He made me feel a little better about my rash decision to call 911 and explained that if this had been a serious fire, opening the front door could have caused a serious oxygen draft and made it much worse.

The chief stated that in 2014, there had been an arson case in Toledo that killed two firefighters. It happened because a door was opened, which caused a surge of flames. I remembered this—our Girl Scout troop sent cards and hand-drawn pictures in remembrance of those who were lost. The owner of the apartment building was later sentenced to twenty years in prison for a crime that cost two very good men their lives. It was not nearly long enough, in my opinion. The fire took two fathers and two husbands, all for an insurance payout. I didn't know these firefighters personally, but I still think of them every January.

I felt bad calling these brave firemen to my house, but I was forever thankful it turned out okay and that all my children were safe.

I have never lived through a true house fire. My dryer went up in flames and now my oven had too, but everyone was safe. There was minimal damage, and we still had a roof over our heads. Not all families have been this lucky. I recall as a child hearing about a devastating fire that happened to some of our distant relatives. Afterward, my mom asked if I had any toys or clothing that I would be willing to part with to help the family out. I had no toys that I *wanted* to give up, but I bagged up my Barbies, Cabbage Patch dolls, and some other odds and ends. I was only ten years old, but I remember clearly the day when we dropped off the items at their empty temporary apartment.

They had lost everything—down to a tattered, well-worn sock without its match, a well-loved teddy bear, and all their photo albums. EVERYTHING! Could you imagine?

Teach your kids fire safety, do fire drills, and instill in them a respect for fire. Teach them to err on the side of caution. I must admit that I have not always been so diligent, but hopefully my kids will know what to do in an emergency. When something scary does happen, panic takes over. In the two fires I have experienced, I forgot most of what I knew. What I did remember was to get the hell out, call 911, and don't be a hero.

Did you know that every eighty-eight seconds, firefighters respond to a residential fire, and the leading cause of those fires is cooking? Smoking comes in second. Each day, seven people die in a house fire. My simple mistakes could have been catastrophic. The repetition of practicing and going over fire safety with your children is so important, because some information will be retained.

Just before I published this book, a good friend of mine set her kitchen on fire while cooking. She has been living in a hotel for five months with her husband and four children while they are redoing her entire kitchen and most of the first floor of her house.

October is national fire safety month. Change your batteries and check your smoke detectors. Practice fire drills. Make it fun... bake cookies and stop by your local fire station to drop them off. They always love to show kids around and talk about fire safety. Make it a family fun month full of fire safety activities and games. Stop by my blog betsyharloff.com in October to find a list of fun activities to go along with fire safety month.

CHAPTER 10

Baked Turtle with a Side of Overstimulated Mouse

Pets will come and pets will go, and I have made my share of mistakes bringing pets into our household. Some lived happily ever after...and unfortunately, some did not.

The unfortunate thing in life is that in order to learn, you must do, and sometimes someone or something gets hurt. Those are hard lessons. Those lessons are never forgotten.

THERE IS NO SUCH THING AS A FREE PET

Sure, you can get an animal for free when someone you know has a pet that has babies. However, the supplies a new pet will need will cost a pretty penny.

When Sebastian was two and a half years old, my neighbors inadvertently bought a cute, fat, and very pregnant guinea pig from the pet store. The difference between fat and pregnant can be hard to discern; I have made that mistake a few times and once even put my hand on a friend's belly, asking her when she was due...but she wasn't pregnant!

Imagine the surprise of waking up to a cage full of itty-bitty, newborn guinea pigs just a week after they brought their new chubby pet home.

I was convinced to come check them out, and as an animal lover, I fell in love with the guinea pigs right away. So did my little boy. How could he not? At the time, my son was having a lot of nightmares and saying there was a boy in his closet. He also had an imaginary friend he talked to sometimes, and that friend sometimes scared him. I later found out that a child had hung himself in our garage before we lived there. Really creepy, if you ask me—maybe my son sees dead people. They say you are more open to things like that when you're young.

We ended up picking out a white guinea pig with pink eyes and dark grey ears. Joe was not thrilled, but we did it anyway. Joe went on and on about how much money our *free* guinea pig would cost us, with the cage, the bedding, the food, the water bottle, the toys, and so on.

We named our new pet Superman because he was a super guinea pig with powers to protect him and keep the "noisies" away. The noisies was what Sebastian called the strange sounds in his closet and in his room at night. Superman's cage was right alongside his bed. Sometimes Sebastian would fall asleep with his cute little face pushed up against the wire cage as he watched Superman scurry around and chew on his Quaker oatmeal cardboard house. Every time Sebastian was scared and heard a noise, we assured him it was just Superman and that if anything scary did come into his room at night, Superman would fight them. It worked. Sebastian started sleeping more soundly and felt safe in his bed.

Superman moved to a few houses with us and lived a very happy, long life. He didn't die until he was ten years old. The average life span for a guinea pig is 4–8 years, and every other guinea pig from that litter had died at a very young age. He really did have superpowers.

It's funny that he was with us for ten years, but he's only a small blip in my memory. I remember that when he heard a crinkling bag that sounded like baby carrots, he would squeal until he got one. His cute white face would later turn orange from the beta carotene that stained his white fur.

When he did pass, we buried him under the large scarlet oak tree in our backyard. As with any death, it was hard, but we had a gathering at the gravesite and all took part in burying dear Superman and saying our goodbyes.

AQUATIC SNAILS

After we had moved to our large piece of land, which included a decent-sized pond, the kids had fun exploring all the creatures that lived there. They found many species of frogs, a variety of water bugs, painted turtles, and a plethora of tiny pond snails the size of green peas. I found them out there one morning having a race to see who could gather the most snails. Between the three kids, they had more than fifty snails. They were not nearly as big or as beautiful as the vibrant apple snails we had bought from a pet store. These snails were varying shades of muted brown, excellent for camouflage in the wild.

My oldest daughter asked if she could add a few of these snails to her fish tank because they were so cute. I didn't see a reason why not. She joyfully plopped in a few, while we watched to see what they would do. They did nothing, not right away at least. Just a few hours later, however, they were moving all over the tank.

"Guys, come look! They're all moving!" Alexis shouted into the rec room so everyone could come check it out. Joe had just come home from work as everyone raced down the long hallway of our house.

"What are you guys running down the hall for?" he asked.

"The snails I put in my fish tank from the pond are moving around," she replied.

"Well, you better watch them now because they aren't gonna survive in your tank. They'll be dead in a few days," he said confidently.

The joke was on him—or maybe the joke was really on us, because not only did they survive, but they thrived!

In just a few short weeks, they tripled in size, and Alexis noticed something strange on her tank. There were tiny spots all over, like something had splattered on the glass. We soon realized that the speckles on her tank wall were moving. Our pond snails had hundreds, maybe even thousands, of babies in a small ten-gallon tank. There were so many that we scooped a bunch out to study them under a magnifying glass, then put them back into the pond.

The kids wanted to keep a few and watch them grow. I saw no harm in that, so we left ten or so on the glass. Little did we know that there were still hundreds on the pebbled aquarium floor, completely camouflaged. As they grew, we realized we had missed a bunch. We scooped snails out daily and threw them back into the pond. It was a never-ending supply of snails.

This went on for a few weeks. No matter how many snails we scooped out, we never got them all, and the water in the tank got dirtier and dirtier. We finally decided we needed to dump the whole tank. We managed to save her neon tetras and her Kuhli Loaches, which are cute bottom-feeding fish that look like baby eels with whiskers.

During this whole ordeal, Joe just shook his head in exasperation, wondering why I kept trying out new pets even though it always seemed to end badly.

I don't think it was horrible, though, unless you were to ask me on the Saturday I spent five hours cleaning the tank! It was quite the learning experience, and how many other children can say they bred and cared for baby snails?

As I was writing this chapter in 2019, the kids and I were studying snails, using a study curriculum created by a wonderful mama over at www.raisinglittleshoots.com. It's a great resource for homeschool or traditional school families who want to embrace nature and learn more about the natural world. During that week, we went on snail hunts, sketched snails from nature books, and painted ceramic snails. We were hoping to find one in nature to study, but it was just too cold for land snails. Instead, we headed off to the pet store to purchase an aquatic snail. While we were in line to pay for our new critter, the kids took turns holding the bag and excitedly peering in at the golden snail shell. I reached the register and realized I had left my wallet at home. The snail was only $2.99, but I had no cash.

After a quick trip back home, we were able to make it to the pet store before it closed to bring our new friend home. She is rather shy, but we enjoyed learning about mystery snails—they're pretty cool!

BED-TIME BUDDY

Just after we bought the house we currently live in, located on fifteen acres, we had an incident with an American toad. You see, we had no idea we were going to buy a house. Joe and I both saw this property go up on auction the same week, but we weren't looking to move. We had a plan to move in five years. But fifteen acres with a pond, a bunker, woods, a barn, and a woodshed just minutes from the city seemed too good to be true. We got pre-approved at the bank and knew exactly what we could afford.

On auction day, we were the first to arrive. I pulled my youngest from her car seat and wrapped her in my lightweight gauze wrap so I could keep my hands free. The house was a strange 1970s ranch, complete with gold, orange, and dark brown wallpaper. (I currently have a love/hate relationship with this wallpaper—it's still up in our entryway.) Nothing had been updated, it was like walking back in time to the 1970s, and it was dirty. But there was no major damage, and we could move in after a good cleaning.

I paced through the house for over an hour while they did the contents auction outside. I envisioned what it would be like raising a family here. That ugly, dirty house felt like home to me…it felt right. Dirty and outdated, but right!

There were hundreds of people at the contents auction happening outside, but only forty or so people in the house for the house auction. There were only a handful of active bidders, and Joe and I had no idea what we were doing, but a small woman who welcomed us to the neighborhood helped us along, explaining that her and her husband flip houses. Then, just like that, we unexpectedly won our dirty, ugly house on fifteen acres. Thirty short days later, we started a new chapter of our lives.

We were not at all prepared for how long it was going to take to get our current house packed up and ready to be rented, plus get the new house cleaned and ready to live in. We spent every day at the new house for the first week, scrubbing floors, ripping out shelving, and clearing out all the extra stuff left over from the auction. We didn't get all of it. In fact, as I write this, the attic and some bookshelves are still full of stuff from the nice gentleman who built this house in 1969.

While we worked on the house, the kids spent all day exploring our fifteen acres (except for the baby, who I wore in a soft structure carrier on my back while I cleaned). They especially loved the pond, which made me very nervous because a few were non-swimmers. They also quickly discovered that we had a very large toad population. Just about every time they lifted a log or paving stone, they would find a toad nestled underneath.

After one long day, we packed up our coolers and headed back to our small house in the city. I didn't know that my two youngest boys, aged six and seven, had smuggled a large toad into the van. I should've known something was up when they were very well-behaved and especially quiet.

Once home, they quickly took off to their upstairs bedroom. I thought they were just happy to be inside after spending the last nine hours outside. I should've also known something was up when they never bothered me about when dinner would be ready. While I reveled in the peace and quiet, the boys were upstairs playing with their new friend, the toad.

Dinner was over and baths were taken, and I got ready to head upstairs to tuck the boys in and read them a story.

"You don't have to read tonight, we're really tired," Xander said.

I looked at Tyler, who shook his head in agreement. I shrugged and said, "You sure?"

"Yup, night." They both raced up the stairs.

This was rather strange behavior, but I was so exhausted that I didn't question it. I thought they were possibly just as worn out as me.

I finished up some chores, then sat in the rocker to nurse Bailey. At 9 p.m., I sent Sebastian, who was eleven at the time, upstairs to bed. The boys shared the upstairs, which was just one large bedroom. He came down minutes later to say, "Mom, there's something croaking in our room!"

"What?" I said with a heavy sigh.

"Yeah, I think there's a toad in our room. I think the boys brought it home from the other house."

"No way! How would we have not noticed?"

I headed upstairs, stood in the dark room, and listened.

Crooooooooak!

That couldn't be a toad, could it?

Crooooooooooak!

"Okay, who has the toad in here?"

Xander slowly pulled back his blue monster-printed comforter so I could see the softball-sized toad resting in a small nest made of blankets.

"Where did it come from?"

"The other house."

"In the van? How did I not hear it the entire drive home?" I asked, exhausted and confused.

"Sebastian told us that if we kept him overnight he would turn into stone like a statue, and we think a statue toad would be pretty neat."

How could I have missed this? The signs were all there. They were quiet and behaved on the way home; they stayed in their room playing happily; and they went right to bed with no trouble. I should've known. But you know what? I did know—I knew something was not right, but I was just too exhausted to look further into it. Was it that horrible that they brought a toad home? No. I think it was rather funny and harmless. We put the toad into a container in the mud room with some wet dirt and took him back to the other house the next day.

That night, Xander complained of stomach cramping and vomited. I started to wonder if the toad made him sick. It turns out that the Eastern American toad does indeed emit a toxin from glands just behind its eyes. If ingested it can cause stomach upset or vomiting. Clearly the toad was not ingested, but Xander was a habitual thumb sucker, so it's possible he was touching the toad and then sticking his fingers in his mouth. I'm not sure if the toad actually made him sick, or if it was just a fluke, but it was a great beginning to a conversation about safely handling toads, frogs, and whatever else they could come in contact with on our large property full of wild creatures.

This was not the end of the toad shenanigans. After we moved into the new house, I routinely saw toads hopping across the floor, sometimes after the kids were in bed. One night I was sneakily eating my favorite dairy-free mint chocolate chip ice cream while watching *Grey's Anatomy* on Netflix when I saw something hop across the dim room.

My middle boys would bring these suckers in the house and either forget about them or just leave them because they thought it was funny. There was one unfortunate occasion in which a toad was left in a pocket and somehow made it into the washing machine. Imagine my surprise as I pulled the clean, wet clothes from the wash and out fell a toad from a pair of jeans! The poor toad was nice and clean, but no longer breathing.

BAKED TURTLE

I've never had a pet turtle—the salmonella thing grossed me out—but my friend Lacey did. Sebastian was friends with her son when he was little and enjoyed visiting to see their new pet. It was mid-spring and the weather was just getting nice. We had been over to their house almost every day that week.

The kids were energetically jumping on the trampoline while Lacey and I sat outside at her patio table with tall glasses of ice-cold raspberry sun tea watching the boys when I noticed her empty aquarium.

"Where's your turtle?"

"Oh," she said, looking off toward the bright yellow daffodils popping up in her garden that danced carelessly in the warm breeze. "He died."

"I am so sorry, what happened?"

"I killed him," she said flatly. "You know how it was really warm out yesterday? It was just over 80 degrees, and I thought our turtle would love to bask in the sun and get some fresh air. So we brought him outside and set him on this very table.

"We were outside all day, and around noon when we ate lunch, Jimmy noticed how active the turtle was. It was the most active we had ever seen him. He usually never moves. We thought he was just appreciating this new warm weather, like we were. I had no idea what was really going on.

"When Darnell came home from work, he laughed at the turtle as he walked past with a plate full of hot dogs and hamburgers to grill. He mentioned that he looked like he was living his best life and enjoying the day. The turtle was racing back and forth, trying to climb up the glass walls and madly scratching. Thirty minutes later he was no longer moving, so I lifted off the tank lid and reached inside. I was shocked by the temperature inside. I realized immediately what I had done. I baked our pet turtle to death! That was why he was so active, he was fighting for his life, trying everything he could to get out, until he succumbed to the heat and went off to turtle heaven."

She sat for a moment, remorseful.

I was horrified. What a heinous death. Could you imagine being baked to death?

I'm ashamed to admit that I judged her, and when I came home to tell Joe he judged her as well. He even said to me, "There's a special place in hell just for her!" I thought that was rather harsh, but he had never much liked her, so maybe that tainted his opinion on this entire incident. I kind of agreed, though, it had to be a horrible way to die. But this was an accident, and in no way intentional. Lacey was not capable of that.

KARMA AND THE DUCKS

Throughout my life, EVERY TIME I have judged someone, it's come back to me. Karma is real, and she makes sure that what goes around comes around. But I never see it coming—I'm always blindsided.

Fast forward many years: we bought four Pekin ducks as meat and seven Khaki Campbells as layers. Joe built a coop with a clear roof, thinking that if the roof was clear he wouldn't need to add any windows. You need sunlight in a duck coop so the sun can kill bacteria. Ducks also need sunlight to know when it is night and day. Joe didn't want to bother with the extra work it would take to cut windows, so he thought building it with a clear plastic roof would be great. I was resistant about not having a window because it would be needed for ventilation, but he did make small vents in the walls, so I ultimately just shrugged and went with it because I didn't want to build it!

We quickly discovered that the clear roof created a greenhouse effect, which made the coop HOT! We were new farmers, so we were learning from experience. We stapled a beige tarp to the top of the roof, preventing direct sunlight from getting in, but the coop still got too hot without windows to release the hot air. We knew it was important to let the ducks out first thing in the morning just before the sun came up.

We loved our ducks. I loved watching them on the pond, and set up a hammock so I could enjoy lazy summer days listening to them quack and watching their graceful swimming. Sebastian, who was fourteen, was responsible for the morning farm chores, taking care of the ducks and chickens. When he went away to Boy Scout camp, I took on his chores. One Sunday, he came back very early, just as the sun was coming up. He unpacked his bags and assumed that the animals had been taken care of.

I assumed that since he was home so early, he was back to doing his chores.

Later that morning, I headed to the store to get some groceries and noticed that the ducks were not on the pond. I thought it was strange, but figured they were in the tall grass laying eggs or foraging. My gut told me something was not quite right, but I ignored it and drove on.

When I came back from the store, the ducks were still not on the pond, but I didn't check it out. At dinner, Joe mentioned that he hadn't seen the ducks either, but none of us looked further into it. We have fifteen acres, and the ducks were free range, so we just thought they were off foraging somewhere. It wasn't until after dinner when I went out to check on the garden that I noticed two Pekin ducks quacking and following me, far away from the pond.

They must be hungry...oh crap!

I ran to the coop, knowing just what had happened: no one had let the ducks out, so they were stuck in the greenhouse/duck house all day. I opened the coop, and two male ducks raced out like lightning. The others were not so lucky. One of our beautiful white Pekins had his lifeless head draped over the black rubber water bowl. It was a sight I will never be able to erase from my mind.

My dear sweet feathered friends, who depended on me for survival, had perished because of me! I stormed back to the house, ready to blame my son.

"SEBASTIAN!" I yelled. "Did you forget something today?" I didn't wait for a response. "You never let the ducks out and now they're dead. They were fucking baked to death!" I knew my words were harsher than they should've been. I watched his eyes turn glassy as my words were thrown at him with a vehemence that a parent should never have.

Joe came around the corner.

"You!" I turned on Joe. "You were the one who felt it was too much work to put a window in the coop and put that clear roof on. You created a greenhouse!"

I was in so much pain over the ducks' horrific death that I wanted to blame everyone else but myself. But I knew it was all of our faults.

I put my boots on. "I need to go shovel out the dead from our coop!" I stomped back to the coop with shovel in hand and tears dropping from my eyes. I was scooping out my first duck when Joe came out and gently grabbed the shovel from my hands.

"Get Sebastian," he said with glassy eyes. "He needs to help with this and take responsibility for what was done."

The three of us somberly cleaned the coop, scooping seven lifeless ducks into the wheelbarrow. We were silent, avoiding eye contact because the sadness in each other's eyes was too much. I lifted the heavy wheelbarrow, pushing it toward the woods and feeling the weight of what had happened. We never talked about this event again until the day I wrote the book currently in your hand. I called Joe at work to make sure the details were correct. As I was hanging up, he said, "Let's never speak of this again."

Looking back, I know it was unfair of me to blame my son or Joe. I had my part in it too. I was the parent; I was the adult. I should've made sure that Sebastian did his chores when he got back from Boy Scout camp. I should've never yelled at Sebastian. It's one of my deepest regrets. I hope I didn't scar him for life; he was only fourteen, and that was a shitty thing for me to do.

That's the thing with trauma. It's so easy to toss blame on anyone but yourself—it's human nature to protect yourself. It's how our minds work; it's how we live with ourselves. Some people live in denial their whole lives, and some people realize what they did and own it. It's harder to deal with emotionally when you take the blame, but it's an essential part in becoming a better person. I didn't learn this until my late thirties when I saw the hurt and pain in my son's eyes.

There were so many signs that day, but I ignored them all. I don't ignore those signs anymore. If I feel something is wrong or off, I investigate. Sometimes that means I call a friend or relative out of the blue and just ask if everything is okay. Sometimes I go back in the house to make sure the dryer is off, because I know

I always follow my gut now. I NEVER IGNORE THOSE FEELINGS. MAYBE THIS ONE HORRIBLE MISTAKE HAS PREVENTED ME FROM MANY OTHERS. *maybe that's just what I tell myself.*

they can start fires. Sometimes I get back out of bed after I'm in pajamas to head outside to the barn and check on the animals.

But sometimes I don't want to be inconvenienced.

It will be fine. It will be okay.

Then I see that beautiful white duck with his head draped pitifully over the water bowl. It wasn't fine that day; it wasn't okay.

I always follow my gut now. I never ignore those feelings. Maybe this one horrible mistake has prevented me from many others. Maybe that's just what I tell myself.

THE LOSS OF OUR FIRST DOG

I am thinking of the song "The House that Built Me" by Miranda Lambert. In the song, Lambert sings about a visit home and the spot in the yard where her favorite dog was buried.

The kids picked a good spot to bury our first dog, on a hill next to a tree by the pond looking at the house, so he would never be lost. He was wrapped in blankets and buried with his purple leash because he loved walks, some treats because he loved to eat, a football because he loved playing tackle with Sebastian, and a balloon on which Xander had drawn a face. The kids said their goodbyes, and they all helped put dirt over him at his final resting place.

I had never wanted a dog. I am not a dog person, but this dog stole my heart.

He was my first dog, a pureblood black lab. I bought him for my husband, but that stinkin' dog picked me as his owner. Funny how animals do that! I tried to get him to sleep with my three-year-old son, but that bull-headed dog refused to sleep unless he was by my side.

For eleven years that dog either slept in bed with me or right next to my bed. When I was in labor with my kids, he knew before I did—he would follow me around the house and whine.

We have lost a few dogs over the years and slaughtered a variety of well-loved farm animals for food, but none have touched my heart, or my children's, like the death of our first dog.

WE'RE GONNA EAT OUR DOG

Speaking of slaughtering animals for food, when my youngest was just four years old we were at a pet-themed library story time when my daughter announced that she too had a dog and some cats, then said, "But we're gonna eat them soon."

The librarian stopped, speechless, then looked at me.

"Well," I laughed, "we slaughter and eat our ducks, chickens, and pigs on our farm, but we do not eat our dogs or cats."

Clearly, I needed to do some clarification with Bailey on what was food and what was a pet. I will never forget the look on their faces, though!

Animals enrich our lives. They bring us joy, they teach us responsibility, and even provide us food sometimes. I remind my children when we slaughter one of our well-loved farm animals. We gave them a happy life, they felt love, knew what kindness was, and were able to roam happily at our farm grazing on all sorts of goodies, which is more than we can say of their factory-farmed relatives.

The animals that have graced our lives have taught us many lessons, including some very hard ones. They filled our hearts with joy and sorrow. Mistakes have been made, some at a great cost, but lessons were also learned.

CHAPTER 11

The Momtrum—
Also, Known As the
Mom Temper Tantrum

In a perfect world, we would all speak in soft and calming melodies and never raise our voices—but this isn't a perfect world. The people closest to us know how to push our buttons best. This is why siblings fight so much—they know where all the buttons are—and our kids know where our buttons are too!

I wish I could tell you that I never yell, but I do! I've been on the phone with friends who had to set the phone down in order to yell at their kids, only to apologize for yelling because they say that I'm always in control and never yell. Ha! Not true, and I quickly correct them. It's comforting to see other moms lose their cool because it helps me feel like I'm normal. I've never met a mother in my twenty years of parenting who hasn't lost their cool and snapped at their kids. We all lose control, and we all regret it.

FREAK OUT IN THE CANDY FACTORY

We were on a tour of the Spangler candy factory in Bryan, Ohio, with over thirty homeschool friends. Spangler makes candy canes, circus peanuts, lollipops, and many more items. We rode through the factory in a trolley sporting stylish hair nets for a behind-the-scenes tour on how they manufactured, stored, and packaged these goodies. The kids laughed as we rode under a conveyor belt carrying wrapped lollipops, a few falling onto the floor as we rode past.

After the tour, we were escorted to a small gift shop full of candy and other novelties. It was almost lunchtime, so kids and moms alike were hangry. A chorus of children begged for all sorts of candies. We usually eat fairly clean, but I let my kids pick out candies to sample. Life is all about moderation. As I stood in line with a group of other moms waiting to purchase sugary snacks laden with red dye #40, I saw my friend Nellie struggling with her son.

Nellie is a mom of three. I had known her from cloth diapering, baby wearing, and breastfeeding groups, but we were not friends until she started homeschooling.

She once told me that when I showed up to babywearing meetings with my oldest son, who was six years old at the time, she thought I was a weirdo because I homeschooled! The irony is that she's a weirdo homeschooling her kids now too. This has happened with more than one mom I've met. Oh, karma, the games you play!

Nellie was an introvert. She kept very quiet, observing her surroundings and not interacting with others unless she knew them. I thought she was a snob before I got to know her. She had a soft and quiet voice, but today her voice was loud and assertive as she struggled with her son. She was scolding him and telling him he was not allowed to have candy. He was not taking no for an answer, so their voices got louder until he screamed at her.

Up until this point, I had been watching out of the corner of my eye, but when he screamed at her, we all turned to look. She roughly grabbed his arm and guided him outside. The glass doors were not soundproof, and although we could not fully hear

Sometimes you have those days

THAT EVERYTHING BUILDS, AND EVENTUALLY YOU JUST FLIP OUT, USUALLY FROM THE SMALLEST THING.

It's not the small thing that caused the anger;

IT WAS THE BUILDUP OF SMALL THINGS ALL DAY LONG

what she was saying, we could hear yelling. We all understood her tone and body language. She was mad!

We paid for our items, pretending not to pay attention. We gave each other that raised eyebrow look of knowing—she had lost it and was having a Momtrum. A few minutes later, she came back inside, collected her two other children quickly, said a quick goodbye, and left abruptly.

It was comforting to see this mom, who always looked so calm and together, lose her temper with her child. I think it made us all feel more normal. We could all sympathize with her and her child, because we had all been in her shoes.

Sometimes you have those days that everything builds, and eventually you just flip out, usually from the smallest thing. It's not the small thing that caused the anger; it was the buildup of small things all day long. I believe this is how Momtrums usually work—at least that was how it worked in the next two stories.

THE DANCING CHRISTMAS TREE

It was just after Thanksgiving, and I had pulled out all of the Christmas decorations. We had accumulated a fairly large collection of dancing, singing plush decorations. My mother-in-law started buying them for us because the kids loved them. I had just found out we only had three left, because I had forgotten to take the batteries out before packing them away the year before, so battery acid had exploded over most of them.

I was having one of those days that everything went wrong. Joe needed a favor; the kids were fighting all day; the bank screwed up a deposit; I stained my favorite shirt; and I forgot about dinner, burning it and setting off the smoke alarms.

Just after I finished dinner (round two, which did not get burnt), one of my children came around the corner swinging the top of the dancing plush Christmas tree and banging it carelessly on the walls.

"What the heck are you doing?" I shouted. "That's not a toy that we play with like that! You're going to break it and dent the walls!"

I was yelling so loud that Joe and the rest of my children filed in to see what the commotion was all about. I snatched the toy away and said, "If you don't want to treat items with respect and play with them properly, then I'm going to throw it away."

I'm not quite sure what I was thinking, but I threw the dancing Christmas tree down the hall with such force that a black plastic piece flew off and hit the wall.

"Well, it didn't seem broken until you threw it down the hall," replied Alexis, who had mastered the art of sarcasm from listening to Joe and me.

I turned to glare at her, knowing she spoke the truth and even more angry that my child had calmly stated the obvious. Joe saw my look and quickly ushered the children out of the room before coming back in to find me fuming and fighting back tears.

"Are you calm yet? I think you're overreacting," he said.

Of course I was overreacting, but now I was even more mad at myself for losing control and yelling at my child for mistreating a toy, then breaking it myself. This was not a great parenting moment. I took a few minutes to calm down, then called the children into the room.

"It's not okay to yell and throw things, but even adults sometimes have a hard time containing their emotions or acting appropriately," I said. "I'm sorry that I yelled, I'm sorry the dancing Christmas tree is sort of broken. It still works, but the lid that holds the batteries just snapped. We can just tape that on."

We still have the dancing Christmas tree, and I'm reminded of this episode every holiday season when I see it sitting on the shelf.

SUMMER IN SUBURBIA

A good friend recently told me about a Momtrum of her own. Here's her story:

It was a pleasant sunny day, and I had spent the morning scrubbing, decluttering, and reorganizing my kitchen. I felt quite accomplished, so I decided to reward myself by putting on my new swimsuit so I could lay outside on the deck working on my tan while my son played in our fenced-in suburban yard. It was a very skimpy, two-piece black bathing suit. The sun felt so good against my skin. I closed my eyes relaxing while the sun's rays penetrated my entire body, soothing my sore muscles from a morning of housework. A gentle, cooling breeze carried the sound of a distant lawnmower, birds chattered in the trees, and I could hear my son Oscar crashing his trucks together in the grass. Life was good!

I was startled when my husband abruptly opened the slider doors and stood over me. "What the hell are you wearing?"

"I think it's rather obvious," I replied sardonically.

"I told you that I did not want you wearing that swimsuit out here when the new neighbor is outside."

We argued for some time before I finally got up and stormed into the house to change clothes. I was so irritated that he felt he could tell me what to wear. I threw on a pair of whitewashed, distressed jean shorts and a black graphic tee before heading downstairs to make lunch. As I rummaged through the fridge for some cold cuts and a salad, I was faced with the realization that I had to go to the grocery store.

I pulled into the store parking lot, shocked to see it so full. Why was everyone at the store? Ah, it was the weekend before the Fourth of July, so everyone was getting all their barbeque and grillin' fixins. I helped Oscar unclip the buckles on his car seat while he grabbed his tattered, sage green blanket.

Fighting our way through the store, I was tossing food in our cart hurriedly when Oscar started sobbing. "I lost my blankie."

"Do you know where?"

"No." He sniffled.

That blankie was everything to him, so we spent an extra twenty minutes zig-zagging through crowded aisles. We eventually found the blankie right in the entryway of the store. I snatched the blanket and headed back in. I was hoping to get everything I needed in one trip so I didn't have to come back tomorrow.

"Mom, can I get a new car?"

"No!"

"Mom, can I please get a new car?"

"No, stop asking," I responded again, irritated. I was trying to remember everything I needed and still annoyed with my husband.

Trying a new tactic, Oscar yelled, "Mom, get me a toy now!" People turned to look.

"NO!" I yelled back just as loud.

"I HATE YOU!" he screamed.

That one stung. I don't care who you think you are, those words hurt. I was feeling overwhelmed and embarrassed, so without thinking I yelled back, "I hate you too!"

I pushed the cart to the checkout with Oscar tantruming the entire time about the toy car. I refused to give in, knowing that if I did, he would learn that the bigger tantrum he threw, the more stuff he got. I had given in plenty in the past, which was why he was having such a fit right now.

My child is trying to break me!

I loaded everything on the conveyer belt. As the cashier scanned the items, she made eye contact with me and said, "I admire your patience and ability to not give in, I know how hard it is!"

This gave me a little boost, knowing I wasn't alone. I felt utterly alone right now! I pushed my cart outside with Oscar still screaming. A woman loading groceries into her trunk stopped and glared at us as we strolled by.

I got everything packed up, jumped in the car, and pulled out toward the road. It was now past lunch, so I decided Chick-fil-A would be good for a quick meal. I was in no mood to prepare a lunch.

Oscar realized we were in the drive-through and started screaming, "I want a strawberry shake!" I ignored him while he kicked the seat and flailed about, demanding his strawberry shake. This continued the entire drive home.

I pulled into our attached garage and refused to help my screaming child get out of the car as he demanded I unclip him. I carried in the groceries, put them away, and laid out his food before going back to the garage to help him unclip. I was hoping the tantrum would wear him out and he would be over it by the time I returned.

I was wrong. He waltzed into the house, throwing his blankie onto the floor, and took a seat at our white farmhouse table. The moment he realized there was no strawberry shake and that his cup was filled with lemonade, he started crying again. "I'm not eatin' nothin'!" he yelled, shoving his food away.

After eating just two nuggets, I slammed my barbeque sauce on the counter, sending the dark red sauce flying up to the ceiling. I stormed over, snatched up his lemonade, nuggets, and fries, and said, "Fine, have your fit, now you'll be hungry!"

I stormed into the kitchen, dropped his food into the trash, and threw the cup of lemonade across the kitchen into the sink. The lid popped open mid-air, sending ice and lemonade all over the freshly cleaned kitchen.

I stood there, just staring at the mess. I had snapped.

My son looked over at me and said calmly, "I'm calling Dad and tellin' him you're acting *crazy!*"

*****

My friend had lost it, just like myself and many moms before her. It was again the accumulation of many little things until she just blew up.

Parenting is hard AF, and that mom at the grocery store knew it. That's why she tried to support my friend the best way she knew how. It only takes a minute and a few kind words to let other mamas know that none of us are picture-perfect. We need to show each other more support and less judgment. Failure doesn't make you a bad mom—it makes you a normal mom.

DIRTY LAUNDRY

Just after we moved into our new-to-us old house, raw sewage backed up into the house and through every drain, including the kitchen sink. We needed a new septic system. (It took months for me to feel comfortable washing dishes in the sink, and that was after I soaked it with bleach for days at a time. Would you want to wash your dishes in the toilet? That's how I felt about my sink after seeing noxious brown liquid oozing up.)

This happened in the middle of winter in Ohio, and the ground was frozen. The plumber, a family friend, was going to do the work for us, but we needed to wait until spring when the ground was softer.

We learned to be very conservative with our water, not wanting another backup. The septic tank was in good shape, but the leach field was bad. The liquid waste could not move out fast enough, so when the tank was full, it was full!

We had a 1,250-gallon tank, which seems big, but not when you factor in seven people showering, flushing the toilet, and using the sink for cooking, teeth brushing, and so on. We eventually disconnected the pipes under the sink to drain into five-gallon buckets so less water would end up in our septic tank. We would then dump these buckets in the woods. We had to learn a new way to live, and we learned how wasteful we really were with our water.

I had to start washing our clothes at the laundromat. At first, I took all the kids with their schoolwork during the day, and we did our lessons there while the laundry did its thing. But my youngest was always running around being crazy, and it was quite the nuisance.

Some days after Joe was home from work, I would go by myself, make the best of it, and bring along a book. I learned to enjoy the quiet time, my mini momcation.

One cold, snowy February, I'd been avoiding hauling the laundry to the laundromat for much too long. Joe was home, so I made plans to head to the laundromat by myself.

At 7:45 p.m., I hauled three large hampers of dirty laundry to the van and headed out. Having seven people in a house creates a lot of dirty laundry. I would have just enough time to get it all washed and partly dried before they closed. I could still use our dryer at home, so sometimes I only washed at the laundromat and hauled everything home to dry. Other times I dried and folded it all there. Today would be a rush because they were closing soon.

I sorted the laundry, poured soap, and plinked my coins into the machines. I then sat down on one of the plastic black laundromat chairs to read. There were quite a few people there...working moms, bachelors, and an elderly couple. Sometimes I would sit and make up stories about these people and what their lives were like. That night, I was distracted from reading my book by a very loud adolescent boy who was yelling random things and slamming the dryer doors.

The other patrons were whispering to each other and staring. I suspected he was autistic, and since he was a teenager, I could only imagine the mood swings his mom had to deal with. Having my own teenagers at home, I was well aware of the ticking time bombs they could be with all those hormones running through their bodies.

Before long, Roselee, the staff attendant, walked up to the mother and said, "Excuse me, but you need to control your son. He cannot walk around slamming the doors."

The mother went over to her son, grabbed his arm, and said, "You need to calm down. You cannot act like that."

He jerked his arm away and ran from her like a toddler, dancing and yelling, "No, no, no!"

She chased him and dragged him outside for a talk. I could hear them yelling through the glass. She walked back in and headed back to her laundry. I had my book up, trying not to look, but I couldn't help it. She had on a pair of jeans and a faded pink sweatshirt. Her wavy brown hair fell to her shoulders, and she kept tucking her hair behind her ears as she folded. She must have felt me staring. Her gaze met mine, and I smiled warmly at her. She returned a half smile, but she looked so worn out and defeated. This is the mom face we hide. The moment was ruined soon: her son was shouting obscene rap lyrics.

"Hey!" Roselee shouted. "You need to control your child."

An older woman in a lavender cardigan spoke up loudly, "This is what's wrong with kids these days. They have no discipline." She pushed her cart of fresh laundry to a folding table near a gentleman with a blue plaid shirt. "Ridiculous!" she said, making no attempt to lower her voice. He nodded in agreement, put his reading glasses back on, and then went back to his Sudoku puzzle.

"Noah, stop that right now!" his mom yelled.

"NO ONE LIKES ME! FUCK OFF!" he screamed at her.

She looked down at her laundry with tears in her eyes, while her son skipped between the rows of washing machines, yelling.

"You're gonna need to leave if you can't calm your son down," Roselee said with her hand on her tiny hip, standing firm and with authority, her mild Southern accent sounding stronger.

The mother walked near her son, trying to talk to him, but it turned into a yelling match. No one was even trying to hide the fact that they were all staring. Her son seemed highly volatile... she was clearly exhausted and at her breaking point. She walked back to her laundry, pulling clothing from the dryer and forcefully throwing it into the basket. She turned to look at everyone staring at her and shouted, "He won't listen to me! He's troubled. His father couldn't handle it and left us last month. I don't even know how I'm going to make this work anymore."

I knew I needed to do something...but what? This woman was clearly overwhelmed. I didn't want to overstep, but I felt like I should act.

What should I say?

A man in his late twenties wearing baggy pants cinched at his hips with his red boxers showing turned to her as he walked out the door with his olive green military style laundry bag and said, "Woman, you need to beat his ass and take control."

Wow, beat this kid? That's the solution?

This kid was clearly autistic or had some other disorder, his father had just left them, and he shouted that no one likes him. He was hurting.

I got up and walked toward her, unsure what I was going to do or say. She looked up from her laundry defensively. I took a deep breath. "You're doing a great job. I have five children, and I know it's hard. People are quick to judge and say harsh words, ignore them." I hugged her.

She started crying. "Thank you," she said. "Thank you so much!"

She poured out her life story to me in a fast, sobbing rant, getting it all off her chest. I just stood there and listened, nodding. I offered no advice, only my ear. What she needed most at that moment was to be heard. Even though we were strangers, we had one thing in common: we were moms. I could relate to her struggles and failures. Mine may look different, but they had one underlying theme: we both thought we were failing our kids.

As I listened, I noticed her son watching us from a distance. His mood changed abruptly as he watched his mom break down into heavy sobs as she poured her story out to me. No one wants to see their parents cry; it affects us all so deeply on an emotional level. I can only guess as to what was going on inside his head, but I saw sadness and remorse on his face.

He walked over to a chair, pulled out a small neon green bouncy ball, like the ones you get from quarter machines at grocery store exits, and proceeded to bounce it. He sat there without saying a word, but remained fidgety as he repeatedly bounced the ball, trying to catch it in different ways. At one point he even fell from his chair, but got right back up and continued to bounce his ball.

"Five minutes till closing!" Roselee shouted, pulling her sandy blonde hair back in a ponytail and starting her closing duty tasks.

"I need to go grab my laundry, hang in there!" I said with a slight nod and a smile.

I loaded up my wet laundry, planning to dry it at home, then lugged my hampers full of heavy, wet clothes to the van. I smiled again at the exhausted mom before I walked out the door and noticed her son now helping her with a basket heaped with folded towels. Sometimes we just need someone to listen and say a kind word.

I think about her when I drive past the laundromat, wondering if I could've helped her in a better way and also wondering how she and her son are doing.

Momtrums happen. Just because we are grown-ass women doesn't mean that we can't scream, cry, and just break down from the heaviness of it all. Sometimes it's that breakdown that causes us to see the light and correct course.

CHAPTER 12

Wine, Whine

I have always had a love/hate relationship with alcohol. I like the buzz, that fuzzy feeling you get after a glass or two of wine. It quiets my mind but leaves me in control. However, I don't like to be drunk. I have obsessive compulsive disorder, so my brain never settles down. It's in a constant state of chaos. When I drink, it stops the incessant counting and pattern-finding, but most of all, it calms the broken record in my brain of whatever I happen to be obsessing about currently.

I don't drink every night, and sometimes I go months or years without a drink, but the more stressed I am, the more my OCD flares up and the more I drink. I have tried prescribed medications, but they quieted my mind so much that I was emotionally numb. I felt nothing...no joy, no sadness, I just existed.

I knew I could not live a full life staying emotionally numb, so I chose to stop taking the prescribed drug Celexa, and before I could try another option, I got pregnant with Alexis, my second child. Overjoyed to find I was pregnant after just three months of trying, I knew I would not want anything in my body that wasn't nourishing to my second miracle baby. I was told from a young age that conceiving children would be near impossible, but here I was, pregnant with child number two.

For me, it's easy to refrain from alcohol or any drug when I am pregnant or nursing, because my baby comes first. No judgment to that mom who still indulges in a glass or two of wine when pregnant or nursing. Studies have shown that it's okay in moderation. I just choose not to because moderation is a hard one for me when it comes to alcohol.

I truly believe we are all doing the best we can as parents and I respect the choices of others, even if they are not the same as mine.

I WILL HELP YOU, MAMA

In my mid-twenties, when my youngest was just three years old, I worked in a nightclub. Guys bought me drinks all the time, but I learned to pace myself and to only ever just have a slight buzz. I needed to be able to count money and be quick with math, a skill I never mastered while drunk. I had key words that let the bartender know to lighten the alcohol in my drinks, so it smelled of alcohol to the poor chump who bought it but I didn't get drunk or lose control.

While I worked there, a friend and coworker of mine was getting married—I was to be her maid of honor. On the night of her bachelorette party, we all piled into the limo, which was fully stocked with loads of hard liquor for a night to remember—or possibly not remember.

We were a group of scantily dressed, attractive, twenty-something ladies in miniskirts and six-inch stilettos. As we spilled out from the limo at each venue, we attracted plenty of attention.

Guys flocked to our group, happy to buy us drinks, hoping for a chance to party with us.

"Why aren't you drinking, Betsy?" asked my friend Nikki, a tall, dark-haired beauty.

"I don't like to drink that much, just enough for a buzz. I will have a shot or two, but I don't like getting drunk."

"If I'm drinking, you're drinking too!" yelled Ashley, the bride-to-be, who usually never drank but had already consumed way too much.

Just before we reached our third bar in downtown Toledo, Ashley jumped outside the limo and threw up next to the curb. The line of people waiting to get into the club all turned and looked. As I held her hair back, our limo driver walked up to the front of the line to get us in without waiting.

He returned just as Ashley was fixing her lipstick and popping a stick of spearmint gum in her mouth to cover the stench of vomit and alcohol.

"You girls are all set to go right in, I will be waiting right out front."

The nightclub was just filling up, and the constant thrumming of the bass made it hard to talk. It was dark, and smoke from the fog made the lights cutting through the smoke look like samurai swords. Working in a nightclub ourselves, this was a familiar scene. We headed straight to the bar, ordered a round of shots, then proceeded to the dance floor.

I was already feeling a bit beyond buzzed, and with all the commotion no one noticed that I started tossing the liquid over my shoulder instead of down my throat. It's easy to fool drunks; I have had lots of practice where I worked. Now I was just fooling my drunk friends into thinking I was drinking as much as them.

I kept this up at each bar, only doing shots when everyone did them as a group and there was no way they were going to let me out of it.

After hitting up a few after-parties, I finally arrived home at 4:30 a.m., drunk and high from a joint I smoked on the ride home. Don't worry, I wasn't driving. I was feeling confident that I wouldn't get sick after avoiding so many shots, but I still consumed more than I should have.

I woke up just a few hours later and spent the next hour emptying my stomach into the shiny white toilet while the room spun. I had fallen asleep on the bathroom floor, still dressed in what I was wearing the night before.

Sebastian had just woken up for the day and walked into the bathroom very concerned. "Mommy, are you sick?" he asked, sitting next to me in his adorable yellow fireman pajamas.

"Yes, Mommy is a little sick…don't worry, you can't catch what I have."

"Oh, how come you so sick then?" he asked.

I have never dumbed anything down when talking to my children, so I said, "Well, sometimes adults drink alcohol. It's a liquid that makes them feel funny, but if you drink too much you can end up getting sick and your body makes you get rid of it to protect itself."

"Oh, you shouldn't drink that stuff then."

I shouldn't, but I did, and now I feel like crap while my three-year-old states the obvious!

I stood up to get a small drink of water and was shocked at the image staring back at me from the oval mirror hanging over our pedestal sink. There was dried vomit in my hair, and my face looked like an abstract art project. The black mascara and eyeliner that had been so perfectly applied the night before was smeared across my eyes in a dark blur, creating a hauntingly death-like appearance. My eyes were puffy and bloodshot, my cheeks were red and blotchy, and lipstick was smeared up my face. I looked like something from a horror film.

Oh God, how could I look this bad in front of my baby? No wonder he looks so concerned. I bet he's terrified. Heck, I'm a little scared by the image looking back at me.

I grabbed a washcloth from the linen closet and started scrubbing my face, but the sudden commotion sent my body into a fit of dry heaving.

"Mommy, you okay?" he asked, crying and patting my back.

Oh God, my reckless, irresponsible night is going to scar my poor child.

"Yes," I managed feebly between earth-shattering heaves. "I'm going to be okay."

After my stomach quit having spasms, I grabbed my wet washcloth, walked to the carpeted hallway just outside the bathroom, and laid down in the hall with the cool washcloth on my head. I heard Joe come up the creaky stairs, a murmur of talking, and then silence.

Sometime later I woke up to Joe standing over me. "I'm heading off to work, Sebastian ate some cereal, and he's watching *Blue's Clues*. Do you need anything before I go?"

"No."

I wished he would have stayed and taken care of me, showed me some compassion, showed me that he cared for something more than just his company. I knew deep down that he did and that all this work was for us to have a better life, but I was so lonely. Weekends meant nothing to him—it was just a normal workday. There was no relaxing; it was just work, work, work. Not everyone has the grit to put in the time to start something new and hope that all the time and effort will pay off. Joe did, but at a very high cost.

Later, my eyes fluttered open to the pleasant sound of Sebastian happily playing with his Matchbox cars in the hallway next to me. He noticed me stir and said, "Hi, Mommy. I brought you a pillow and a glass of water."

This sweet little boy is so worried about his mama, and I feel like a complete piece of shit, as this illness that has my son so worried was self-induced.

"Thank you so much, sweetie, you are such a big boy!" I said in my cheeriest voice.

I laid there listening to him play quietly next to me, thinking there were hundreds of little boys and little girls all over the country right now taking care of their mamas because they were sick from drinking too much. I have read a few memoirs about this exact situation, when children were forced to act like adults and the parents acted like irresponsible children. Now I was laying on the ground with my head pounding while my son took care of me.

A tear slipped from my eye, then I drifted back to sleep. I woke again to see Sebastian sitting there munching on a box of Cheddar Bunnies.

That poor child, he was so hungry that he just fixed himself some food and stayed here with me, afraid to leave my side.

"Once you're done with those crackers, it's nap time. I will lay with you in your bed."

I snuggled next to him on his full-size bed, breathing in his sweet little-boy scent. I'm not sure who needed the comfort of each other's company more. We fell asleep, safe and warm under his blue sailboat comforter, and slept peacefully. By the time we woke up at 3 p.m., I was feeling well enough to start moving around. I showered, dressed in fresh clothing, and made my way to the kitchen, where I pieced together a dinner of chicken nuggets, mac and cheese, and green beans. I still felt pretty woozy, so I passed on this basic American-mom dinner. I just drank orange juice instead. I was able to push through the rest of the evening watching movies on the couch with my favorite little guy, but I didn't pay attention. My mind was obsessing over what a horrible mom I was, getting so drunk that my three-year-old felt the need to take care of me and worry about me all day.

I did not drink for over a year after that, not one drop. I've never forgotten the day that my three-year-old took care of me.

MOMS NIGHT OUT BOOK CLUB

I wish I could've gone out more when my kids were younger, because hanging with friends and remembering that I am an independent person as well as a mom is revitalizing. Being able to enjoy food at a leisurely pace without having to stop and wipe someone's butt, refill a sippy cup, break up a fight, or search for a favorite toy is awesome!

I host a local book club, which has turned into a moms night where we chat about life more than whatever we're reading. Not everyone even reads the book...no judgement, I get it. Everyone is on their own path and has their own priorities.

A few months ago at my book club, we met at a local Starbucks and I was asked a few questions about this book.

"So, what's it about?" asked a mom I had only met twice before.

"Well, it's a book of imperfections and parenting mishaps. I am putting it all out there because I feel that with perfect images always being thrown at us in social media posts, it's hard to

We are all flawed,
YET WE CHOOSE TO ONLY
SEE THE GOOD IN EACH
OTHER WHILE WE RIP
OURSELVES APART.

Believing we are not good
enough at the one thing
another mom is good at.
WE ALL HAVE OUR
STRENGTHS AND OUR
WEAKNESSES.

We are all uniquely
different, but we are all
good moms.

remember that we are not all as picture-perfect as the posts make it seem. Does that make sense?"

She nodded.

"Just like I feel when I look at your homeschool Instagram feed," my close friend Liz said. This was a shock because she knows so many of my failures. Why would my feed make her feel inadequate?

"What? Why?"

"You're so good at homeschooling. You're always posting pictures of things you are doing with the kids, and you're so much better at it than me. You got your son into college at fourteen and your daughter at eleven, and I just enrolled my kids in public school because I couldn't do it as well as you."

This made me sad, because there I was posting pictures to help inspire others and it was doing the opposite.

"You know," I said, "you do so much with your children. I see it on Facebook. You take them everywhere and offer them so many more experiences than I give my children. You always find the greatest money-saving deals and off you go. I often look at your pictures and think you're a better mom than I am."

We all laughed, realizing that as we all sat drinking our coffee in Starbucks, we were all feeling inadequate as parents. We all know we are good parents, yet we still felt that pull to compare ourselves with others.

"THIS!" I shouted, standing up. "This is why I'm writing this book, right here, right now. We are all sitting here comparing ourselves to each other. We are all flawed, yet we choose to only see the good in each other while we rip ourselves apart. Believing we are not good enough at the one thing another mom is good at. We all have our strengths and our weaknesses. We are all uniquely different, but we are all good moms."

The conversation hopped around, but eventually landed on being frustrated with our children. I mentioned that sometimes in the middle of our school day, I need to pour myself a glass of wine to ease my nerves. The very perfect-looking mom sitting across from me drinking her coffee from a clear mason jar with a homemade rainbow knitted coozie spoke up, "Sometimes I need to have a shot or two of gin at 10 a.m. to get through the day!"

We all seemed a little shocked at this confession, but soon we all chimed in to say that we had also indulged in a little alcohol in the late morning or mid-day on very hard days to keep from snapping. A splash of Bailey's Irish cream in a morning coffee, a shot or two of gin, a glass of wine, some vodka mixed with orange juice…we have all been there. It's okay to admit we are all not so perfect. In fact, we should all let each other know that we are just as flawed as the next mom.

DAY DRINKING RULES

Day drinking seems to be taboo no matter what your age, no matter what you do. There's something about the end of the day that makes it more acceptable to crack open a beer or enjoy a glass of wine. Also, if you're drinking with others, it's acceptable to sip on a margarita, but not if you're drinking alone. There are just so many unwritten rules and taboos about day drinking, I cannot even keep up. Who made these rules up anyway? Rules are just general guidelines—if you want to drink at 10 a.m., do it! Just be responsible and do not get drunk or drive anywhere.

Last summer I was invited to an impromptu summer playdate at a friend's house. She set up some inflatables and got out water balloons, squirt guns, and a volleyball net. We were instructed to bring a dish to pass and share. If we couldn't bring a dish, she told us to just show up anyway. It was mid-summer, the days were hot, and our kids were complaining that they were bored.

The counter was laid out with a fruit salad, a veggie tray, spinach dip, guacamole, pico de gallo, chips, pretzels, juice boxes, and sparkling water. We all plopped our stuff on the patio and grabbed a seat around her patio table under a giant umbrella. I sat in the shade, because I'll burn if I even think about the sun.

Some of the other moms chose to sit in the sun, propping their legs up to soak up the rays. It didn't take long for all the kids to start playing while we sat around and chatted. I heard the loud whirring of a blender coming from the kitchen. A moment later, my friend popped out with clear orange solo cups with bright neon straws sticking out. "Anyone want a frozen strawberry margarita?" she cheerily asked.

"Yes!" a chorus of moms cheered—except for one mom who didn't drink. It's funny how people fully respect it if you don't drink, but if you do drink, friends always seem to pressure you into having just one more. Why is that?

HOT DAYS AND HARD CIDER

"C'mon, guys, let's head outside," I yelled to any kids still in the house. They grabbed their sandals and followed me out. They pulled out scooters, bikes, and sidewalk chalk and busied themselves playing on this hot summer day. I sat barefoot on the cement steps just outside the kitchen in my pink, knee-length flowered skirt, sipping my cold drink, enjoying the hot sun on my skin. I called this skirt my naked skirt—it was a two-layer, modest, gauzy skirt that was so thin and cool I felt naked in it. I wore it on especially hot days.

I finished my first hard cider, then went into the house and grabbed another. I walked down the driveway in search of some shade. I was walking under the maple tree in front of my house, my toes in the cool dirt, when I saw my neighbor Ali across the street walk out her front door and start heading my way.

"Can we play across the street with our friends?" my children asked.

"Sure," I replied. I rounded up my kids to cross our street together barefoot, bottle still in hand while I reminded them to look both ways. We didn't live on a busy street, but sometimes cars do fly down the road.

Ali looked at me, pausing at my feet. "No shoes today?" she chuckled.

"Nope, I had only intended to sit on my front steps watching the kids play, but then it got hot in the sun and the cool dirt felt good on my feet." I looked down at my feet; my dark red toenail polish was a stark contrast from the grey dirt covering my toes.

"Oh my," I said, laughing. "I guess I'll be scrubbing my feet when I go back inside."

"What are you drinking?" Ali asked.

"Hard cider."

"Oh," she said with a pause. "I didn't realize you drank. I've never seen you drink before."

"I do. Every so often, I go through cycles. Would you like one?"

"No, we don't drink in our house."

"Oh geez, are you a recovering alcoholic? I can go dump this out, I'm so sorry," I responded, feeling really bad.

"No, no, nothing like that. I used to drink before I was married, but now that I'm a born again Christian, we choose to not consume any alcoholic beverages or eat at places that offer alcohol."

"Oh, wow, I've never heard anything like this. I was raised Catholic and my neighbors growing up were Christian, but I had no idea that Christians don't drink."

"Not all Christians choose not to drink, this was our choice."

"But why?" I asked.

"Well, the Bible talks about how alcohol can cloud your judgment and bring forth unholy carnal desires."

"Seems pretty accurate," I snickered. "I had no idea, thanks for sharing this." I looked down at my bottle and wondered if it was making her uncomfortable. I was raised to be respectful of other people's choices. "Is this bothering you?" I held up my beer. "I can dump it out?"

"No, it's fine."

I guess I won't be inviting her over for margaritas.

Throughout my life I have been friends with people of diverse cultural and religious backgrounds. I feel I can mesh well with just about anybody, and I'm always intrigued and genuinely curious about others' views and beliefs. People really like to talk and explain their beliefs to others. Some even like to have friendly debates with me.

WINE THIRTY

Wine thirty is around 3:30 or 4:30 p.m., that critical time of the day when moms and children are melting down. Kids are hungry and tired, and their whining has reached its peak. Siblings are fighting. For me, this is the worst time of the day. I'm exhausted both mentally and physically and very much need a break. Friends of mine have husbands who will be arriving home to eat dinner and help with the evening rituals of bath time, dinner, dishes, and toy clean up. Not me, not today, not any day...my husband will not be home until after the kids are in bed. He wants to be around us, unlike our first year of parenting, but he's just busting his butt building a better life for us with his company.

This time of day always seemed like the best time to drink. There are only a few hours left in the day and the bedtime battles are looming. Having a glass of wine while I cook·dinner helps the whining become a little bit more tolerable.

As soon as dinner is ready and I put food in my stomach, it absorbs all the alcohol anyhow. But on some days, the hard ones, I have a second glass while keeping an eye on them in the tub. I will push around the bathtub boats and help make lavender-scented bubble beards on their tomato-sauce-stained faces. But on the really, really hard days, I will have a third glass of wine while I read *Goodnight Moon*, *Corduroy*, and *Llama, Llama, Red Pajama*, sometimes falling asleep right alongside my children.

If you want to have a drink to ease your nerves, do it. If you want to have a drink because it tastes good, do it. If you want to drink to calm your mind, do it. And if you choose to not drink for any reason, do not feel bad about that either.

You do you, boo! Just be smart—if you do decide to drink, do not drink and drive, and never get more than just a very light buzz if you're the only adult around. If a child was ever going to do something reckless, it would happen if you were drunk. Maybe that would be my luck! How would you get your child to the ER? Call an Uber?

DRINKING WINE IN THE BASEMENT

I was at the library with my children—my oldest daughter was volunteering for the summer book club. While I was browsing for books, I came across a familiar little girl. Her arms were full of books, with her head just peeking over the top.

"Hello, how are you? You may not remember me, but I'm your mom's friend. I come over sometimes after you're in bed to hang out with her."

"Oh, yeah, she has people over all the time. I'm supposed to be in bed, but I sneak down when no one notices and listen," she said very matter-of-factly. She reminded me so much of one of my children. Although she was young, she spoke as if she was twenty years older, like an old soul stuck in a little person's body.

"You've got a great stack of books there!"

"Yeah, I like to read," she said.

"I love reading too," I said. "Well, have a great day, it was good running into you. Enjoy your books."

I continued browsing, looking for books while my children played in the newly renovated library. The library now had new touch screens with pre-loaded games, an ample supply of child-size computers, and a Montessori play area. Everyone loved the new branch for the bright and engaging children's area. It was a very popular spot on hot summer days.

I walked past the new seating area next to the children's area and saw my friend chatting with another mom.

"Hey," she said, getting up from her chair. She had long, dark hair like her daughter and was very petite, maybe not even one hundred pounds. Despite her petite size, she was gorgeous and had birthed three babies from her tiny frame.

"I ran into your daughter and had a great conversation with her. I wasn't sure if I freaked her out at first because we've only met a few times, but she was chill and talkative."

"She's not shy, that's for sure," she responded.

We chatted for a few minutes before she had to run after her youngest child, who was currently fighting over a plastic chicken leg near the play kitchen. I gathered up my things, checked out my library books, then rounded up the four children I had brought with me. I saw my friend's daughter playing at the same popular touch screen as my youngest daughter. "It's time to go, Bailey, say goodbye to your friend," I said.

"Bye! I gotta go," Bailey said, looking for her rainbow purse. She took her sweet time walking toward me. I think she hoped that if she moved slow enough, I would change my mind and just let her stay.

"Bye," I said to my friend's daughter. "Tell your mom I said bye too, we have to get going."

It took her a few minutes to respond, as she was very engrossed in her game. I was halfway to the door and a good twenty feet away when she stood up, turned my way, and shouted, "Bye, I'll see you next time you come to my house and drink lots of wine with my mom in the basement! I'll try and sneak down and say hello."

I was cracking up, as she had just called out her mom and me in a quiet library. Now everybody was looking at me, the basement-dwelling wine drinking mom. I didn't mind; I've been called much worse.

MOMMY JUICE

We don't drink a lot of juice in our house, so when I do buy juice the kids are very interested in it. However, if there is juice in the house, there's a 50/50 chance that I have spiked it with Malibu Rum or my favorite brand of tequila. My kids found this out the hard way, by sneaking sips of my juice cups only to find out it tasted bad.

"Mom, there's something wrong with the juice on the counter," one of them would say.

"Well, if you're talking about the blue mason jar, that's mine, and it's mommy juice."

"What's mommy juice?"

"It's regular juice that I add alcohol to. Children are not supposed to like the taste of it. In fact, it's illegal to drink it if you're under the age of twenty-one."

This is the terminology I have come up with for any spiked juice or drink. Over the years, I started putting my "mommy juice" into wine glasses so my kids will know from the cup they shouldn't be drinking it.

My kids have asked to taste it from time to time, and I've let them have small sips every now and again because I feel that curious kids are more dangerous than ones who are never exposed to alcohol. I want my children to ask me things they are curious about without fear. I'm not telling you to give your kids alcohol. I'm telling you that *I've* let my children at various ages try small sips of alcohol, not to get drunk but to fill their curious minds with information.

No matter what you call your alcoholic drinks, just be sure that your kids know that it's not okay to sip any alcoholic drink without parental consent.

COFFEE, ADVIL, AND WINE— MY TRIFECTA TORNADO

A couple years back, while writing the middle of this book, I got stuck in a vicious cycle. I would wake up early in the morning to write and finish an entire pot of coffee. Not only was I writing a book, I was homeschooling four children, taking care of a farm, dealing with the sudden loss of my last living parent, and trying to maintain a clean house.

I was struggling, and my stress levels were high. I started drinking while I made dinner four to five days a week to lower my stress. At first it started with the boxes of wine I had brought home from my dad's apartment after he died. After I drank it all, I started buying more, enjoying the relaxing numbness. Soon after, the headaches started. I was very dehydrated from all the coffee and alcohol, so I started popping lots of Advil. A year or so into this coffee/wine/Advil trifecta, my stomach started to feel the burn, literally.

I didn't know it at the time, but all the pain and stomach issues I was having weren't from a lingering stomach bug that had hit our house repeatedly in the early spring of 2019. It was actually damage to my stomach lining.

I was in so much pain one Sunday evening that I could hardly move. I knew I needed to see a doctor, and luckily I was able to get an appointment for Monday. I had been seeing this doctor for a long time, and she knew my aversion to most drugs and that I ate a very clean diet.

By the time I saw her, I was vomiting, having irregular stools with blood in them, and so bloated it looked like I was five months pregnant. I was also burping all the time, and it felt like my stomach was on fire.

She couldn't figure out what was wrong, but as she was making her last notes, she turned to me and asked, "You haven't been taking any painkillers, right?"

There was a long pause.

"Well…yes, I've been taking a lot of Advil. If I'm being completely honest, I've been popping them like candy."

"Oh!" She was shocked by my admission and looked me right in the eye. "That can most certainly tear your stomach up and cause internal bleeding, especially with the other issues you're having. Have you been drinking at all?"

"Yes." I paused, embarrassed. "Wine. Usually a few glasses… more than a few times a week."

She shook her head, very concerned. "Are you drinking coffee as well?"

"Yeah, about a pot a day. I usually drink coffee all morning, have a light snack, drink wine while I write in the afternoon, and then drink more wine with dinner, which I only nibble at, then I take some Advil."

Despite the fact that I had been eating very little, I hadn't lost any weight because I was drinking my calories.

She had me lay down on my back again, poking around my abdomen as I winced when she hit all the right spots.

Presently,

**THE MOM CULTURE IN
OUR SOCIETY IS TO**

*drink, and
drink often.*

Be smart, ladies,

AND KNOW THAT WINE

*is not an accessory
to motherhood!*

"Your pancreas is enlarged," she stated while continuing her examination. "You are heading down a very dangerous road." She reached out her hand, helping me to a seated position. She made some notes on her computer, took her glasses off, set them on the counter next to her laptop, and then turned to me.

"Betsy, you gotta stop!" she said, putting her hand on my knee. "If you were just doing *one* of these things in excess, it could be a problem, but you are doing three! You're tearing up your stomach and have hardly any lining even left. Go back to your herbal teas, stop drinking, don't take any more Advil. If you absolutely need something for the pain, take Tylenol. It's gentler on your stomach."

I left with a prescription to lower my stomach acid to allow for healing...but the healing that really needed to happen was emotional. I did this to myself with poor behavior, poor habits, and ignorance.

I recently read the book *The Power of Habit* by Charles Duhigg, in which he writes about the science of habit, including how to create new ones and how to drop the less desirable ones. This book helped me kick my bad habits. I'm no longer popping Advil like candy, and after my stomach was mostly healed, I re-introduced coffee in moderation. I now reward myself with a cup or two of coffee on Sunday mornings while I chat with Joe. Green tea is my current go-to, and for an extra special treat I head to Starbucks for a green tea matcha latte with coconut milk.

As for alcohol, every time I am stressed and want to reach for a drink, I go exercise, even if I was already at the gym that day. When I do make the choice to drink, I ask myself why I want it and if it's worth it...and it never is.

Presently, the mom culture in our society is to drink, and drink often. Shirts like the one my friend wore at our summer get-together declare "It takes a Vineyard and a Village," and mugs on the shelves of your local stores that state "Mama needs her wine" have made drinking seem like an accessory to motherhood.

Alcoholism is real, and it doesn't always look messy and sloppy. It can look like an ordinary mom who has a drink every night while dinner is cooking. I'm not suggesting that you're an alcoholic if you choose to drink, but I am saying that alcoholism can take on many forms, and just because all your mom friends are doing it doesn't mean you need to do it too. Think twice before you reach for that wine bottle. Is it worth it?

High-risk drinking is defined as more than three drinks in a day or more than seven total drinks in a week. Alcoholism in women is on the rise, and more woman are dying from liver cirrhosis than men. According to the National Institute on Alcohol Abuse and Alcoholism (NIAAA), there was an 83.7 percent jump between 2002 to 2014 in the rate of female alcohol disorders. Astounding, right?

Be smart, ladies, and know that wine is not an accessory to motherhood!

CHAPTER 13

OH CRAP!

Random fact: an unpeeled banana left on the floor by a toddler feels just like a nicely formed log of poop as it squishes through your toes in the middle of the night while walking with a restless newborn.

Before you became a parent, did you ever think that you would become so interested in poop? I never gave it a thought. I mean, really? Who thinks of poop? New parents, that's who! As a new parent, you often wonder if your baby is pooping enough, if it's the right color, if it's the right consistency, and why haven't they pooped in two days?

Babies poop a lot! Sometimes I felt like my babies pooped more than they peed. I quickly realized that the fastest way to get any baby to poop was putting on a fresh diaper or starting dinner. The worst is when you have your coat and shoes on, ready to head out the door, and you hear the messy, watery, gurgling sound of what is sure to be an up-the-back, total blowout kind of poop.

In raising five children through the diaper stage, I have found that cloth diapers seem to hold in these super poops better than their disposable counterparts, but neither are fun. When it does happen, you need to make the very difficult decision of whether to pull the onesie over the baby's head, smearing poop all over your baby, or pulling down the onesie, possibly stretching it to the point of ruining it. The last option is to just cut it off with surgical scissors. After five kids, I have become a master at assessing this crappy situation and knowing just what method is best.

Sometimes I thought I had it all figured out. I would get extra confident and a little cocky. This led to some very crappy situations.

MAKESHIFT DIAPER MAYHEM

Late one afternoon, after Sebastian's nap, I grabbed him and my purse for a quick run to the store. I only needed one item, a missing component for dinner. What I thought was going to be a simple, fast trip turned out to be quite the opposite.

I headed straight into the store knowing exactly where everything was, grabbing the missing ingredient and a few other staples.

As I stood on my toes reaching for the last item from the top shelf, I heard gurgling. It sounded like a bubbling brook coming from my baby. I had no idea we were slowly sailing up shit creek.

Great! I have no diaper to change him. I will just quickly check out, then hurry home.

I heard it again, but much louder as I reached for a box of dried pasta. I turned to look at my twelve-month-old sitting in the cart in a brightly colored fish-print cart cover I had purchased on eBay.

The acidic odor hit me first...we all know that sick smell of diarrhea. Funny that a mom can just sniff poop to know if it's going to be a messy one. Or maybe that's just my superpower. How shitty is it to be gifted the superpower of knowing by the smell of poop if it's solid or runny? You get what you get...at least I have a superpower.

I looked down and was mortified to see a small pool of brown liquid on the floor under my cart. My eyes moved up to my baby's pudgy thighs: they were streaked with brown liquid.

Oh no!

I lifted the back of his sweatshirt. Immediately my hand was wet with warm, watery diarrhea. Not only had this explosion caused a leak down his legs, but it had shot up his back as well, saturating his white onesie to the point that it looked like a dirty brown rag used to clean up spilled espresso in a Starbucks. I wiped my hand on the cart cover on the side not yet covered in human feces.

I looked around to find help. I didn't want to just walk away and leave poop on the floor, but no one was around. I rummaged around in my purse for something. I came across a few tissues and placed those over the top of the poop on the white floor.

That will have to do.

I headed down the aisle toward the bathroom, stopping to let an employee know there needed to be a cleanup by the pasta. Just before I entered the bathroom, I grabbed the half-dozen non-perishable items from my cart and set them on a nearby shelf. I didn't think I was going to make it to the checkout at this point.

I tried to wrangle the cart into the bathroom, but it didn't fit. I decided I should leave it just outside the door. I threw my purse over my shoulder and carefully picked up my child, trying not to get any poop on me. That didn't work. I quickly realized that I was going to be covered in shit.

I cringed as I held my baby tight to my body, grabbed the cart cover, and headed inside the bathroom. I managed to pull the plastic changing table down off the wall with one hand, then placed the cart cover down and put my baby on top. I start peeling saturated layers of clothing off him, fighting back the urge to vomit. I dropped the dripping onesie into the trash, wondering how this much came out of my baby and why on earth the brand new diaper didn't seem to hold much of anything.

Then I opened up the diaper. Every surface was covered in liquid shit. There was a pool of it right under his boy business. I carefully slipped it out from under him and placed it in the waste receptacle, careful not to spill. I had no wipes and no extra diaper, so I used paper towels to clean him as best as I could. The sink was on the opposite side of the room—I couldn't reach it, so I made do with dry paper towels, wiping and absorbing what I could.

After I got him mostly clean, I looked for his clothing. His shorts were covered in shit, so I tossed those aside and grabbed his shirt. I layered paper towels on the sweatshirt and tied it around him, forming a makeshift diaper.

I smiled a little, feeling slightly proud of my ingenuity. I rolled up the shopping cart cover, grabbed my purse, and put my shirtless, mostly diaper-less baby on my hip and strolled out of the bathroom.

I stopped by the cart station at the front door to grab a few disinfectant wipes. I tried to wipe down my hands the best I could while holding a half-naked baby in a makeshift sweatshirt diaper.

Thankfully, it wasn't below freezing. It was a chilly, sweater weather kind of day. As soon as the cold air hit him, he screamed. I was only wearing jeans and a long-sleeved navy blue scoop-necked Henley, so I had no extra clothing to warm him.

We reached the car, and I laughed as I saw our reflection and my sad excuse for a makeshift diaper in the car window. His boy business was hanging out, and I had to take extra precaution when clipping him into his car seat to ensure that I didn't pinch any exposed sensitive areas of his body.

I turned the heat on full blast for the ten-minute ride home, with Sebastian screaming the entire way. I was carrying him on my hip up the three flights of stairs to our apartment when he released his bowels again with a large grunt. My homemade diaper didn't do much to hold anything—shit seeped down my hip and saturated my shirt.

Feeling the warm wetness ooze onto my skin, I thought this, right here, is how being a mom makes you strong. I did not drop my child or scream in disgust, I just unlocked my door, saying many bad words in my head, and marched straight to the bathroom, where I quickly stripped off my clothes and tossed them onto the floor.

I turned the water on and jumped in with Sebastian, rinsing us off and vigorously scrubbing my entire body. Feeling clean enough, I jumped out, plugged the tub, and squirted some soap in to create clean, white bubbles for him to play in.

I haphazardly pulled a towel around my body as I carefully gathered up the soiled clothing and wiped up the mess on the bathroom floor. Before the water was even two inches deep, I glanced over to see it changing to brown. I unplugged the tub, rinsed, and repeated until it was finally clean.

Over an hour later, I got us both dressed and threw together some cereal for dinner, the ultimate busy mom meal. There was no way I was heading back to the store. Joe would not be joining us for dinner, it was usually just my boy and me eating together and enjoying each other's company.

Pro mom tip: always have an extra diaper in the car with a small Ziplock bag of wipes and an extra set of clothing, because that five-minute trip to the store can end in a shitty mess. The Ziplock bag is important because if the wipes are not fully sealed, they'll dry out. This crappy situation has happened to me more than few times with my five children.

Usually the clothes that I use for emergencies are well-worn, stained, or ugly outfits, so they will not be missed in regular rotation. Just check them often in the early stages because babies grow fast, and you don't want to be stuck with a diaper or outfit that's too small. On the other hand, something is still better than nothing.

According to a few surveys, your child will go through an estimated five thousand diapers. Let's say that only one third of those are soiled, which is 1,667, and let's say in all fairness that maybe I only changed half of those, which brings us to 834 soiled diapers multiplied by five children. That brings it to a staggering 4,170 soiled diapers. I have seen a lot of baby shit!

In all those times, though, I have only ever found one yellow Lego head and one wooden blue marble. I've seen plenty of gross poops, but these are the only two times that I ever recall seeing nonfood items that had apparently made their way through the entire human digestive tract. Pretty impressive, if you ask me!

I felt like a bad parent before I did the math, but now I'm thinking this was quite minimal. I kept my house very clean, organized, and picked up. It has gotten a little less clean with each child, and I have often wondered what parents with cluttered, messy houses see in the diapers of their children.

AM I RAISING MONKEYS OR TINY HUMANS?

In September 2013, on my way home from the doctor's office with all my kids in the car, I hit a large black bird—or rather, it hit me. I was driving down the highway at 80 mph when SMACK! Right into my windshield it went. I saw it coming, but I thought it would fly up and out of the way. It never did. My heart stopped, and I jumped at the loud noise. I swerved and almost hit another car. I should have known at that moment this was not going to be a great day.

My middle boys, aged five and four at the time, had been fighting and not behaving all day. After dinner, I sent them outside to play while I folded laundry in the living room. The window next to me was open, so I could hear them as they played with trucks and scooters in the driveway.

My other children were in the fenced backyard with our black lab, Tonka. There was a lot of giggling and screaming outside, which is never a good combo. I thought about getting up to look, but I was just too tired from a day spent yelling at these boys.

At least they're outside. They're probably throwing dirt at one another.

A few moments later, five-year-old Xander came to the door teary-eyed with human feces all over his hands and said, "I'm sorry, Mama, I had an accident."

I was mad, but also felt bad for him because he had diarrhea. So I kind of calmly replied, "How did the poop get on your hands then?"

He shrugged. Now, this was not my first rodeo. I already knew the answer, but I continued asking, hoping that I was wrong.

Please be wrong. This day has just been too much!

"Did you get poop on your hands on purpose and chase your brother?"

They have chased each other before with mud, food, or other items, but have never used human excrement. I guess today was the day they decided to add that to their list.

"Uh…yeah!" he said, grinning as if he was proud of himself.

Calm down, calm down, calm down.

Deep breath.

I opened the door. "Do not touch anything and go stand in the bathtub," I said.

I helped him out of his clothes, making sure to not get shit on anything that wasn't already covered in it. While the shower ran, and he was getting cleaned up, Sebastian came inside. My oldest daughter, Alexis, stayed outside with my four-year-old.

I was then presented with more information about what had really happened outside, giving me more pieces of this poop puzzle.

Evidently Xander had reached into his pants and thrown poop repeatedly at his younger brother while chasing him across the yard.

So that was the screaming and giggling I heard.

Now my four-year-old was standing outside covered in his brother's shit.

Am I raising monkeys? What am I doing wrong as a parent to have my children act like a primitive species?

Sebastian knew I was going to lose my temper, so he quickly stated that he'd cleaned his little brother up as best he could with hose water while I was cleaning up his brother inside.

"Thank you," I said.

Outside, I was at a complete loss for words. There was shit all over the doorknobs, shit on toys, and shit on the garage door.

At least this is all outside and not on my curtains, not on my couch, not on my carpet.

I'm so very thankful that I didn't know right away the extent of what Xander had done, or I might have just lost it right then and there in the doorway of my house. Hearing what happened in stages made it much easier to deal with. I stayed fairly calm through the whole ordeal. Or at least I felt I stayed calm. My children may tell another story.

None of us want to SEE OTHER MOMS FAIL, BUT SEEING MISTAKES THAT OTHER MOMS MAKE HELPS US ALL KNOW THAT *none of us are perfect.*

As I tucked my freshly cleaned children into bed that night, I leaned close to Xander's ear and said, "You know Mama still loves you, even when I get angry with you and even when you misbehave."

His eyes grew wide and he replied, "You do?"

"Yes, of course I do!"

And with a hug and a kiss to each little boy, I closed the door.

I wrote about this in my blog and posted it on Facebook before I took a social media break, and my neighbor across the street responded: "I had no idea they were doing that, I saw them playing outside, but I didn't know they were throwing poop!"

How could she? I'm sure it looked as if they were playing and having a great time. Well, one of my kids was having a grand ol' time throwing poop, but the other child was probably not so thrilled to be pelted with human feces.

She said she laughed so hard that her husband asked her what she was reading. She always felt I was better at mothering in some respects, so when she read this it made her feel good to know that I'm not as perfect as she sometimes felt I was.

None of us want to see other moms fail, but seeing mistakes that other moms make helps us all know that none of us are perfect. We are all flawed and trying to figure out this parenting thing in our own way with our own unique choices. She's a good mom; she has raised her kids with strong Christian values; she never leaves the house without all her kids dressed perfectly; and her family appears to be picture perfect. Are they? No, most certainly not. She has her strengths at parenting and her weaknesses—we all do. We have not always agreed on the way we parent, but we have always respected the fact that no matter our choices, we are both still trying to be the best moms we can be.

I have felt like a shitty parent time and time again. I have been told on occasion that I am a shitty parent, and some days I really was a shitty parent. I have made mistakes that I wish I could take back, but the only thing I can do is learn from them. I don't believe my self-doubt will ever go away. It will always be there hiding in the back of my mind, waiting for the opportunity to squeeze its way to the forefront.

If you are mama reading this book right now, I want you to know you are not alone! Even the most perfect-looking mom has her flaws, and you can be sure that she has made her share of mistakes too!

POTTY TRAINING

Potty training has been my least favorite part of parenting, and I had to do it five times. It's messy, gross, and inconvenient. When I started potty training Sebastian around two years old, I started with disposable pull-ups, but after many months he just used them as a diaper. Then I decided to clear my schedule for a full two weeks and go cold turkey—no diapers anymore, period! The first few days were rough, and I did a lot of laundry. Every time he went to the bathroom, it was in his brand-new Disney character underwear.

By the end of the week, he was making it to the potty 50 percent of the time. Each time he went potty on the toilet, he was rewarded with "potty treats," which were Skittles. Why Skittles? Because I hate them and would not be tempted to eat them. If it was a jar of M&Ms, they would be gone every day, as I would stress eat them thanks to spending the day scrubbing the carpets after the many potty accidents. After two weeks of no diapers, he mastered the potty. It was a grueling week, but it worked. I still used pull-ups at night for about six months or if we were going out for a long period of time. Otherwise, I used regular underwear and brought extra clothes.

It worked so well for my first child that I repeated this same process with my second child, Alexis. I just started earlier, at the age of eighteen months. It took a little longer for her to catch on, but maybe that was because I started her so much younger.

Not too long after Alexis turned two, I was in my bedroom nursing the new baby to sleep while Alexis watched *Elmo's World* in the living room. She was very quiet...too quiet. I have learned that when a room with a small child in it falls very silent, they either fell asleep or they're up to no good. She was up to no good.

I walked around the corner to see her pushing something toward our dog's face. He kept turning away, but she was being very persistent. I couldn't tell what it was from where I was standing, nor could I smell it. Then the baby started screaming, so I went back into the bedroom to soothe him back to sleep. He was fussy and wouldn't sleep, so I put on my Moby wrap and walked back into the room with an exaggerated bounce in my walk to help soothe the baby.

When I walked in, the dog got up and walked to the other side of the room. This gave me a grand view of what had kept my sweet little girl busy for the last hour. She had taken off her pastel striped pants and her cute little pink polka dot panties and pooped on the floor. It was smeared everywhere: the carpet, the TV stand, and the TV screen! This was what she had been trying to feed to our faithful dog: SHIT! No wonder he kept turning his head away.

I stood with a screaming baby strapped to my chest watching my beautiful little girl open and close her tiny little hands as shit squished between her fat little fingers.

I had read about this before from online mommy groups. I recalled a story from many years ago when Sebastian was just a baby. This mama had a child who would paint the walls with poop during naptime. If left alone for too long, he would paint his crib, toys, and everything he could reach with poop.

I was so angry that my eyes welled up with tears. I was not angry at my children—I was just frustrated with the screaming infant on my chest and shit all over my living room. It was a lot to handle.

This was one of those moments you hear about that makes a mom walk out the front door and never come back. Okay, maybe not, but that's how awful I thought it was. How do I clean up all the furniture, my daughter, and soothe a screaming baby at the same time? I don't, that's how.

I took Xander off my chest and put him in the cradle swing while he screamed. Then I bathed Alexis and disinfected everything she'd touched.

Poop painting is a normal thing, and as gross as it is, many kids do it. Fortunately, I only had to deal with this about a dozen times throughout five children.

I know a mom who dealt with this at every single nap for over a year. No matter what she tried, her baby would figure out how to undress and get the poop out of the diaper and all over everything. Her child's room became very minimalist before it was over, because she was sick of washing everything. Thankfully, when she brought her new baby home from the hospital the poop painting had come to an end. I had only dealt with a screaming infant while cleaning poop off everything on one occasion—I can't imagine how hard and frustrating this would have been to deal with every day.

As parents, we have to learn to overcome many obstacles, most of which we never dreamed would be a part of parenting. It's not always glamorous.

WE HAVE TOILET PAPER

At the time of this story, we were living in our Cape Cod house in the city. My three boys shared the large loft bedroom upstairs. This was the only room on the top floor, so I usually only headed up there when tucking children in or cleaning up. This particular day was sheet day, so I trucked up the stairs, picking up a few things along the way and putting them back in their proper places, then stripped the beds. As I was throwing piles of stuffed toys off the beds, I noticed a brown smear on the large plush Stitch from Disney World. It was too large to go in the washer, so I inspected closer, hoping it wasn't ruined. The brown stain was about three quarters of an inch wide and nine inches long. I ran my hand across it and noticed it was crunchy. Still boggled as to what this stain could be, I leaned closer to sniff it. SHIT! How on earth did shit get on Stitch?

"Xander, Tyler, get up here right now!" I yelled down the stairs.

They clamored up the stairs sounding like a herd of ogres, not two little boys.

"Any idea how poop got on Stitch?" I asked.

Did I really expect an answer? I hoped for one, but getting an honest answer when they could tell they were in trouble was rather difficult.

I stared at them, waiting for a response. "You know, poop has bacteria in it that can make you very sick. That's why we wash our hands after we use the bathroom. That way we don't spread germs throughout the house. I can tell this is poop. I'm just wondering how it got there. Anyone care to tell me?"

"Well, it's poop," one of my boys said, hoping the admission of it being poop would be enough.

"Yes, I am already aware of that. What I want to know is how it got there. Did one of you seriously wipe your butt across poor Stitch's torso?"

After a few side looks and hesitations, one of my boys said, "My butt itched, so I scratched it, but I got poop on my fingers, so I wiped it on Stitch."

Oh lord!

"So, you decided to use your stuffed animal as toilet paper? Do any other stuffed toys have anything gross on them?"

The boys walked over to their stuffed toys currently piled up on the floor. They sorted through them, digging and sniffing and then creating a new, smaller pile.

"So there's poop on all of these?" I asked.

"Well, yeah! Or something else," one of my boys sheepishly said.

Something else?

"You guys understand that some of these toys cannot be cleaned properly without ruining them?"

I may have exaggerated a little, but I saw this as an opportunity to weed out the giant pile of stuffed toys that drives me nuts.

"Poop can make you very sick, so to make sure you guys stay healthy I'm going to get rid of most of these. I will wash what I can, but the rest will go in the trash."

A few tears welled up in their eyes as they watched me bag up stuffed toys. I continued to reinforce how unsanitary poop was and how sick they could have gotten. Clearly, they needed a refresher course on wiping properly, with actual toilet paper in the bathroom, to prevent an itchy, poopy butt.

I thoroughly cleaned their room, spending extra time wiping the walls and other surfaces down with bleach water to make sure it was nice and clean. I tried hand-scrubbing Stitch, but all I seemed to do was smear the poop all over him. Sadly, he ended up in the trash.

The takeaway message here is that parenting can be shitty, literally and figuratively, but some deep breaths and some good old soap and hot water can clean things right up.

Parenting can be shitty, LITERALLY AND FIGURATIVELY, BUT SOME DEEP BREATHS AND SOME GOOD OLD SOAP AND HOT WATER *Can clean things right up.*

CHAPTER 14

The Great Outdoors

H₂OH!

The happiest place of all to be is waterside. When I was twenty years old, I moved to Wilmington, North Carolina. This was a very bold move on my part. I knew only one person there, a male friend from high school who I did not know very well. I ran into him when I was in Charlotte, North Carolina, scouting out a place to live. He brought me out to the coast, and I fell in love with the small town of Wilmington.

Two days before I left, my friend Joe, my current husband and the father of my children, stopped by. We sat in my mostly empty apartment with boxes all around, catching up on life, when he asked if he could move to North Carolina with me. He had just lost his job and his girlfriend. He was stricken with deep sadness and just wanted to get away.

I had a two-bedroom apartment waiting for me, so I said sure. I was a little sad that I was no longer going alone. I had wanted to reinvent myself and start a brand new life, and that would be harder with a friend from my past coming along. I'm a strong believer that everything in your life happens for a reason, so I embraced this new voyage with him by my side, and off we went.

My mom drove down with me to help get me settled in. She said how proud she was of me for taking this giant leap and starting over. She grew up without much money in a family of ten and never left the Michigan and Ohio area.

I will never forget the moment my mom first saw the ocean. I parked at the top of the garage at the Shell Island Resort, where I had stayed two months prior while I scoped out a place to live and secured a job. She stepped from the car and looked across the horizon. She took a sharp and sudden breath, and I watched her eyes dilate, dazzled by the expansive ocean. "Oh, Betsy, this is beautiful."

"Yes, isn't it amazing? Do you smell it too? Take a deep breath. Do you smell the salty sea air? That's one of my favorite smells."

"I know why you want to live here. I want to move here now too!"

She spent the next six days with me, walking along the beach and enjoying life beachside. One night during a full moon, I took her out to the beach. The bright moon high in the sky made it look almost like daylight, with moonlight reflecting off the water and sand, creating a bright, magical luminescence.

"When I die, I want my ashes on Wrightsville Beach at this exact spot under the light of the full moon."

"Okay, Mom."

SEBASTIAN'S FIRST VACAY

I only lived in Wilmington for a year. Joe and I ended up together, and he wanted to move back to Ohio to tie up some loose ends. I only agreed because he promised it would be temporary. I had no intention of living out my life in Ohio. Now, twenty-two years later, I am still in Ohio!

While I lived in Wilmington, my childhood best friend came to visit. She quickly fell in love with it, just as I had. She moved in with Joe and me, but she stayed long after we were gone to finish her degree at the University of Wilmington.

She met a man, fell in love, bought a house, got married, and had her first child. So when Sebastian was two and a half years old and my friend's son was one and a half, we decided to fly down to see her and take our boys on their first beach vacation.

I had never been to a beach with a toddler. I was a first-time mom, so I was not prepared for all the things that can go wrong on a beach. Obviously drowning is an issue, so he had on a life jacket and I stayed close by any time he was near the water.

The sand got everywhere, in every crevice, causing redness, chafing, and irritation. I also should have known that sand sticks to sweaty children like glue. He got it in his eyes and shrilled like a banshee as I frantically carried him to the freshwater showers near the parking lots to pry open his eyelids and rinse them.

I also had the great idea to take him into the water with me holding him, but no life jacket on.

I'm holding him, what could go wrong?

It was as if Mother Nature heard me and was like, "Hey, you wanna see what could go wrong?" I was facing the beach, with my back to the waves, so my friend could capture this beachy vacation moment in a picture. As I was smiling at the camera, a giant wave came up from behind me and crashed over the top of us. I held tight to my son, but lost my footing and fell. Sebastian couldn't swim, and the risk of me drowning him was on my mind as I fiercely held onto him while trying to reach the surface. I thought if I let go, the undertow could pull him out to sea. We made it to the surface. Thankfully, he was not unconscious! His eyes were huge and he was coughing. I waded back to shore and looked him over. He was good!

"Mommy, why you do that? I don't want underwater!"

"Oh honey, a giant wave came and I slipped. I am so sorry."

And that was the last time he went in the water that trip. I had scared my poor child so much that he would not let the water even touch the tips of his toes, no matter how much I begged, pleaded, and tried to convince him it would be okay. He walked the shores and collected seashells for the rest of our trip, fascinated by the color and texture variation in each shell. I still have those shells in a box in my closet.

BACK TO WRIGHTSVILLE BEACH ONE LAST TIME

My mom passed away in 2007, when I was pregnant with my third child. Hospice called at 4 a.m., asking if I could get there quickly because she didn't have much longer. I quickly pulled on my fuzzy white and blue maternity sweater and drove through the dark morning hours to the last place I would ever see my mom.

I drove slow, hoping she would be gone already when I arrived because the thought of watching her die seemed horrific. Halfway there, I sped up, realizing how selfish I was being—this woman brought me into the world, the least I could do was be with her as she exited this world.

I made it—she was still alive when I got there. I was met by my dad, brother, and my mom's closest siblings. I sat next to her while she slowly and erratically gasped for air. It was the death rattle. This went on for much longer than I expected…four hours to be exact. We all talked to her and said our goodbyes.

She hung on longer than expected, so we all started telling our favorite stories about her. As the morning sun shined through the window and illuminated my mother like a goddess, I told the story of her first view of the ocean. Halfway through the story, I started talking directly to my mom. "Do you remember the peace you felt as we walked side by side so many years ago with our toes in the sand and waves lapping at our feet. The moon was just above the horizon, lighting up the water like floating diamonds. You are there with me right now, Mom. Can you hear the lull of the waves, smell the salty sea air? It's okay, Mom, you don't need to hold on anymore, you can go. We are all here with you…"

"Betsy!" someone interrupted. "She's gone."

I had promised my mom years ago that I would take her ashes back to Wilmington on the night of a full moon. So that's what I did. We packed up all four kids. By then, the baby I was pregnant with when my mom died (Xander) was four years old, and we'd had two-year-old Tyler as well.

My mother's remains were in the box we collected from the crematorium after her body was done being used for medical research. The trip was bittersweet for me. I loved the ocean and could not wait to share that love with my children, but I was there for a reason. I had a promise to fulfill.

We had a few great days at the beach, and no one almost drowned this time. Sebastian, now twelve, played happily in the waves and had a blast. Thank goodness the near-drowning incident hadn't scarred him for life.

But the time soon came, and the full moon was high in the sky.

Sebastian joined me at the shore at the exact spot my mom first saw the ocean, just below the roof of the Shell Island resort. The night was perfect, with a glowing moon. I took a deep breath and tossed my mom's necklace into the calm water. A surge of waves came from out of nowhere and pulled my mom's necklace out to sea. This was where she wanted to rest.

Her ashes stayed in Wilmington, despite my father's protest at wanting to keep them so he could someday be buried with them. She wanted them there; it was her dying wish. I brought my dad back a bottle of water from the ocean and the metal tag from her bag of ashes so he could be buried with that if he chose.

My dad was put to rest ten years later at Toledo Memorial in Sylvania, Ohio, which was his dying wish. Their physical bodies were not put to rest together, but I am sure their non-physical selves have found a way back to each other in the afterlife.

Losing a parent is indescribable; they're always supposed to be there. I knew they would leave me someday, but I never expected to miss them this much. Even after a decade has passed, I still reach for the phone some days, wanting to call them.

CAMPING TRIP

I grew up taking walks at our local metroparks. I recall the red trail at Wildwood Park seeming like the longest trail in the world—it felt like we were walking for hours. It's only 2.5 miles long! I loved being outdoors with my family and taking in all the sights of the forest. This was my only exposure to nature other than what I saw in my own small backyard. My parents were not outdoorsy people. I think my dad hated the sight of spiders more than my mom, who did all the spider killing in the house. We never did any camping or outdoor adventures. I never even camped outside in our backyard.

When my children grew older, they expressed an interest in camping. I asked Joe if he would try camping with the kids.

"I have no interest in sleeping outside on the ground. Besides, I couldn't get away...I run a company," he said.

I was used to hearing no from him—being tethered to his company was a sacrifice he had to make to be successful. A common misconception about running a company is that you get to do whatever you want. It's quite the opposite. When the boss is away, the employees will play.

My older children have camped in tents with Scouts many times, but I had never taken my children camping solo. I was reminded of the quote hanging in my friend's bathroom: "Do something that scares you every day."

I reserved our campsite at a beautiful spot we had discovered on a camping trip with Girl Scouts a few years back, during the harvest moon. Alexis only wanted to go if she could use her own tent and not be squished in our bigger tent with the three younger children and me.

The forecast called for a few rain showers, but the kids were so excited that I decided to give it a go. Worst-case scenario, we hang out in a hotel or get a room if it becomes a miserable, soggy mess. We headed out very early to set up before the rain hit. I got our tent set up so that I would sleep with my middle boys and my four-year-old daughter, while my oldest daughter set up her own tent.

I sent the kids on a nature scavenger hunt that I found on Pinterest while I made peanut butter and jelly sandwiches and cut up apples. After we ate lunch, it started to rain very lightly, so we all headed to the tent to work on glow-in-the-dark pony bead necklaces and bracelets. The rain let up thirty minutes later, so we emerged from our tents and headed for the lodge.

We spent hours riding bikes along the Lake Erie shoreline with the wind and the breeze of the bay hitting our faces. The sky was a deep indigo with the threat of a nasty storm to the north, but the south sky was streaked with pink and light blue with white clouds floating and the sun shining down. It was breathtaking, a magical moment.

We returned our bikes to the lodge rental station. As I was getting off, my bike felt heavy and pulled to my right, tipping over against the other bikes with a loud thud. I looked over and remembered that Bailey had been in the white plastic bike seat on the back of my bike.

Fail.

"Oh no, Bailey! You okay?" I said, looking at her very shocked face.

I grabbed the bike, hoisted it upright, then unbuckled her and lifted her out of the plastic contraption. I felt so bad—I had completely forgotten she was back there!

We walked inside to pay while the boys lagged behind, still cracking up over the fact that I had forgotten all about Bailey. I approached the counter to pay, but the lady waved her hand and said, "No charge."

"You sure?" I asked.

"Yup, it's slow now that schools are back in session, and I feel bad you guys had to wait so long to get someone to fill up all the flat tires."

"Thank you so much!" I said with a smile and walked away.

"You didn't have to pay?" Xander asked, excited and shocked.

"Nope, she said it was okay. That rental would have cost us close to sixty dollars, so I was pretty excited about her waiving the fee for us."

We headed over to the gift shop, where I picked up a constellation coloring book, a nocturnal animal book, and a few other things before we headed back to the campsite to cook dinner.

I had brought along foil packets filled with frozen meatballs and potatoes. The kids played by the pond right next to our site while I got the fire started and laid out the foil packs. We had them on the fire for over thirty minutes, but they still came out black and charred on the bottom while partially frozen on the inside.

They were barely edible. Xander gagged as he ate his and said it was terrible. There was a strong smoky flavor. We hardly ate anything before we headed back to the beach with our homemade lanterns to watch the harvest moon rise above the bay.

On the beach, there were many other people milling around and waiting for the moon to rise. I played lantern songs on my phone as we walked along the dark shore. Children collected shells and wrote messages in the sand until the clouds parted just long enough for us to see the ginormous orange harvest moon. I tried to snap a few photos, but my cell phone made it look like a small orange blur. The view was amazing; the children were in awe of the sheer size of the moon.

The moon's not actually bigger when it's close to the shore—it's just an optical illusion that makes it look bigger. As the moon reaches higher in the sky, it looks smaller to the human eye. Many scientists and philosophers have theories on why this is, but none have concrete evidence.

After a lot of moon gazing, mostly by me, we headed back to our campsite. I got everybody settled in their sleeping bags by 10 p.m., but I couldn't sleep due to the Claritin D with pseudoephedrine that I had taken that afternoon to help my allergies.

I stayed awake listening to music while I stared at the top of the tent, amazed by how bright it was outside. I had just nodded off when I heard the heaving, wet sound of vomiting. My middle child had just thrown up in the tent. I hurried him out onto the grass and quickly pulled his sleeping bag out. The two other children were still sleeping soundly. It was now 2 a.m., and my sick child was seated in a camping chair and wrapped in a picnic blanket.

"If you feel sick, throw up in the grass or over there in the bushes," I said, pointing just a few feet away. I started building a fire to warm us while I figured out what to do. I could stay and potentially deal with three other vomiting children, or I could call Joe and see if he could help us tear down and leave in the middle of the night. Neither sounded like great options. I didn't want to be stranded there with four vomiting children. Then again, if they were throwing up out here in the grass, it was better than the house!

I decided that we should pack up and head home. I called Joe to come out and help. At 4 a.m., we packed up the van and the truck with all the camping gear and headed back home.

We arrived home just as the sun was coming up, and I started regretting my decision. Maybe I should've waited it out. But then again, I'm not sure how that would have worked out, since his sleeping bag was covered in vomit and currently in our driveway waiting for me to hose it off before putting it in the washer.

Although our camping trip lasted less than twenty-four hours, it was full of memories. Was it picture perfect? Moments of it were, but there were many moments that were not so picture-perfect, including the new coloring book getting soaked, the crashing of my youngest in the bike seat, the vomit in the tent, and packing up to leave in the wee hours of the morning.

None of those moments were picture perfect, yet we had a good time. What I want you to remember is that when you see a perfect photo posted on social media, I'm sure it wasn't as perfect as the photo looks.

OUTSIDE EVERY DAY

Getting kids outside every day is so important—there's just something about fresh air and exercise. Some days it's just thirty minutes when it's really cold or unbearably hot, but on the nice days you will find us outside most of the day.

When I was a younger mom with a few children in a small house in the city with a postage stamp backyard, every morning I saw a very fit blonde woman walking past my window. On the days I was outside in the front yard watching my kids play on bikes, I would wave and we would say a quick hello. She usually had one child on her back in a metal carrier, was pushing a double stroller with two older babies, and one to three smaller children under the age of five walking alongside her. Sometimes these small children were leading the way, and other times they trailed behind.

One summer day, her kiddos saw all our toys strewn across the driveway and came running over to play. She tried to stop them, but I didn't mind and welcomed her and her kids to join us. I enjoyed some adult conversation, and the kids had someone new to play with. She pulled the babies from the stroller and set them in the grass.

"Are all these kids yours?"

She chuckled. "Heavens no, this one here is my grandbaby." She held up the baby. "I run a small childcare business from my home."

"Goodness no, you cannot be a grandmother. You look so young and you're in fantastic shape."

"I assure you I'm most definitely old enough."

"I see you walking every day. How on earth do you get these little ones to come with you? I have a hard time getting my own kids to walk around the block."

"They don't have a choice. Every day after the babies wake up from their late morning nap, we head out. I need to...I have rheumatoid arthritis, and if I don't get my body moving it hurts worse. Some days are really hard because I'm in so much pain, but I need to move as much as these kids do. If I sat in the house with them all day, I would lose my mind.

"These daily walks get me going, which helps my joints and helps to wear them out so they can take a much-needed afternoon nap. If they didn't nap, I wouldn't be able to watch them. I'd go crazy."

"Wow, you're amazing!"

We made small talk for thirty minutes or so before she rounded up her children to head back home for lunch, then a nap. I saw her like clockwork every day. Some days I would wave and see her through the window; other days we would see each other outside.

I wore my own children, using mostly soft-structure carriers. This woman walked every day with an uncomfortable metal carrier that was bad for her back as well as the baby's spine. I had two Boba carriers and an Ergo at the time. I certainly didn't need all three, so I decided she would be the perfect person to give my extra. I looked for her for weeks, but our timing was off until one day I saw her coming down the street with her entourage. I grabbed the carrier and flew out the door; she walked briskly, a woman on a mission, so I knew I needed to move fast.

"Hey, I have a back carrier for you to try!" I shouted.

I explained how this one would be so much better for her and the baby in the most nonjudgmental way I could. I explained that I had an extra one and she was more than welcome to try it out, no pressure. If it didn't work, just pass it along to someone else.

A few days later, I saw her walking past our window wearing the cream and chocolate Boba carrier I had given her with a baby snug inside.

Awesome! It feels good to do good.

As the years passed, I no longer saw her every day. I was caught up in homeschooling my kids and our own adventures, but she never left my thoughts. She became a constant reminder to me to persevere and find a way to go on, even when it literally hurts like hell.

I often wonder how the woman in my old neighborhood is doing, and when I publish this book I will be sure to put a signed copy on her doorstep with a note letting her know what chapter she's in and what an inspiration she has been to me without even knowing it!

WHEN MOTHER NATURE CALLS

When you gotta go, you gotta go. And when you have small children, they don't always give you an adequate amount of time to get to a bathroom. When my youngest was just potty trained, she let me know in the car that she really needed to pee. She had the best bladder control of all my kids and rarely ever had accidents. But she was wiggling around like a crazy animal, so I found the first gas station I could and headed in with my three other children.

"Excuse me, where's your bathroom?"

"We don't have one!" replied a tall, gangly gentleman in a baggy white shirt.

"Seriously? She's two and really needs to go. She won't make it if we drive to another gas station."

"Sorry," he said matter-of-factly.

As I walked back outside into the cool evening air, I mentally went over my options:

1. Drive to another place and hope she makes it. If not, I would have to clean up pee from the car seat.

2. Just let her pee outside in a very public place.

She was crying by then, which was very unusual for her. I decided not to torture her by trying to make it to another store. Instead, I walked her to the front of the car, pulled her pants down, and helped her into a squatting position.

"You want me to pee here?" she asked happily.

"Yup!"

My boys were laughing their butts off and could not believe I was letting her pee outside at a gas station with a parking lot full of people. My oldest daughter, ten at the time, shook her head and looked the other way. "You're going to get us arrested. Is this legal?" she asked.

"I highly doubt any police officer is going to take a two-year-old to jail for indecent exposure, nor do I believe they'll do anything to me other than tell me not to do that again. Which I obviously wouldn't. This was an emergency."

We were on Door Street, which is a pretty busy road just across the street from the University of Toledo, so there were a lot of onlookers.

"People are looking at us," Alexis said, mortified.

"I don't care. They can look. She's two and needed to go!"

A dark trail of pee flowed like a river toward my feet, staining the dark blacktop. It was then that I remembered the very large green smoothie I had shared with her about an hour prior. Green smoothies have a slightly diuretic effect on your body. Her tiny bladder was doing the best it could.

My kids still laugh about this and recall it like it was yesterday. It wasn't my proudest moment as a parent, but nothing in this book is my proudest moment. I should've remembered to have her pee before we left.

We live on fifteen acres of mostly woods. In the summer, when all the trees are fully leafed out, my boys pee outside, and no one can see. In fact, if they try to come inside to pee, I tell them to go pee outside, preferably by the house, barn, or coop. The smell of urine keeps the coyotes away. At least that's what I read, but there are conflicting views on whether this actually works. It's worth a try.

One hot summer day when I was out in the woods with all my little ones building a log cabin fort, my three-year-old had to pee. I looked at the distance to the house and decided it would just take too much time. So I said, "Let's pee outside, I will help you."

She thought this was hilarious and was excited to try. I helped her with her pants and supported her so she could pee onto the leaves and not all over herself. We finished and moved on with our fort building.

Fast forward to later in the summer, and I was giving a tour of our farm to a customer who had stopped by to purchase four dozen eggs. My three-year-old was excited to show another child about her age around our small farm, but then Mother Nature called. My daughter pulled her pants down, and not even squatting, she just stood with a bare butt and peed all over herself and the grass. She then pulled her soaked pants up and continued with her tour.

I was a little embarrassed, but not too much. I laughed and explained to this mother how I had recently taught my daughter to pee outside. I explained that she obviously needed a refresher because she had soaked herself anyhow. The mother laughed and said, "No big deal, I've had to pee while walking on the trail at our Metroparks before, and just went off the trail and peed. No big deal."

My youngest has peed outside many times since then without getting it all over her pants and shoes. It certainly does take more practice and skill for a female to be clean and discreet when relieving herself outside, but it can be done. In fact, I do it quite often when working outside with animal poop all over my shoes. I don't want to trek all the way back to the house when I have woods and no one can see.

Teaching girls how to pee outside is an essential skill, one every parent should teach because when you gotta go, you gotta go!

SH!T HAPPENS

At our old house, I had a friend who took morning walks with me and my children. Sometimes we would stop by a park or play on the local school's playground equipment. On one beautiful, sunny summer day we happened to be playing at a local school's playground when my friend's daughter came up to her mother and whispered that she really "had to go."

"What should I do?" my friend asked. "She really needs to go...BAD!"

"Well, I'd go knock on the school door. I saw some cars in the lot. I bet there are teachers or staff getting ready for the upcoming school year."

She walked to the door, had a short conversation with a stocky, dark-haired woman, and came back to me.

"She says she can't let my daughter in, so I guess I'm going to try and walk back home."

Her daughter was almost in tears and tugging at her shirt. "I need to go NOW!" she said. I felt so bad.

"What do I do?" her mom asked me again.

"Well, I would take her over to the trees and have her go there."

"But she has to poop...she has had diarrhea the last few days," she whispered.

"Yikes, all the more reason I would have her go behind a tree. Do you really think she'll make it all the way home? I would rather my kid poop behind a tree than all over herself on the way home."

She sighed and stared at the trees, weighing her options. Then she said, "Can you distract the other kids while I walk her over there?"

"I sure will!"

She walked off with a very resistant and crying child, who was mortified she had to poop outside like a dog—but when Mother Nature calls, you do not always have a choice.

I distracted my kids and hers with a few games that were spray painted on the blacktop. My friend and her child soon joined us, back from the trees.

"Did she go?"

"Yes," she responded, also mortified. "She didn't want to, but she had a lot of poop. She would've never made it. Should I clean it up or anything?"

"I wouldn't…it's right next to a tree, right?"

"Yes, but what if a child steps in it?" she asked, riddled with guilt.

"Well, it's not like she pooped right on the playground. It's far enough away and next to a tree, so no one should accidentally walk into it. Besides, schools are not in for another month. We're probably the only people visiting this playground. Animals poop outside all the time, and the rain washes it away. Besides, it was liquid, so it should absorb into the ground by the end of the day."

She was so embarrassed that she made me promise not to tell anyone, and I never have—until now. But I will never divulge her name.

THE PEEING CHILD AT A PUBLIC PLAYGROUND

At the age of three, Sebastian once dropped his pants to his ankles and peed right at a public playground full of parents and kids. He didn't even walk far away or turn around. He just stepped off the mulch and peed in the grass, eight feet away from the twisty red slide. I ran over to stop him, but he was already finishing up. I was explaining that his behavior was not socially acceptable just as an adult male walked by and said, "Don't worry about it. My boy has done this many times...it's not a big deal."

I wasn't sure if I should be appalled that his son had done this many times or comforted by the fact that I wasn't alone. As Sebastian grew older, I would let him pee discreetly in public places far off the beaten path where he couldn't be seen.

I have also seen other boys pee in public, either at playgrounds or other very public places where bathrooms are nonexistent or far away. This doesn't bother me at all—as long as the child is under about seven years old. Older children should have had enough practice to know far enough in advance.

My father once taught Sebastian when out adventuring in a place with no bathrooms how to pee into a bottle. I was not thrilled, especially after I discovered some suspicious bottles in his bedroom one afternoon cleaning.

In the case of relieving yourself in public, boys have it so much easier than girls. Girls can do it, but it requires much more finesse. They have to half undress with their rear ends hanging out.

There are so many great parks and play areas, but not all of them are equipped with bathrooms. So, some moms bring along a small potty to use in their vans or cars in an emergency. I never did think of that, until I saw a friend do it after my children had all grown past that stage. Small children are going to have accidents and possibly just pull their pants down and relieve themselves in very public places. It's our job as parents to teach them social norms.

GIRLS CAN DO IT BETTER...
NO, THEY CANNOT

When it comes to peeing in public, I do have a bit of penis envy. It sure would be nice to not have to bare my ass and squat to pee. A friend of mine has been going through an awkward phase with her three-year-old daughter. Every time they get to a playground, she says that her daughter tries to get out of her line of sight to pee behind playground equipment.

"Is she marking her territory like a wild animal? I just don't get it. I have her pee before we leave the house. Fifteen minutes after we arrive, she's off peeing somewhere when I am distracted by my other children."

"You know," I said, "kids do weird things. Try not to worry about it too much. I would just continue having her go potty before you leave, and every time you catch her doing it remind her that it's not okay and take her to the bathroom. After all, she has been peeing in a diaper for most of her life. She might just be adjusting to her new situation."

Sure enough, it was a short phase, and her daughter no longer pees at the playground at the age of eight.

My social media feed is usually full of picture-perfect moments, vacations, achievements, and days. I've noticed that it's in the smaller, more private groups that moms post pictures and talk about their failures. I believe this is because it seems like a safer place, amongst like-minded mothers. I recently came across a post by a local young mother seeking advice about a most embarrassing time. She posted: "Tell me your most embarrassing moment as a parent. My five-year-old girl was playing and climbing with other kids by a tree at the farmers market concert in Perrysburg. She just lifted her dress up, pulled down her shorts, and peed under the tree in front of everyone. Most mortifying thing I can think of to date."

I responded, writing, "Oh my! Bailey did this once when I had a customer over buying eggs. We were not in public, though I will comment later with another example. I have many!"

Two other moms also responded, sharing their most embarrassing parenting moments. We all make mistakes, so I thought for sure that she would get plenty of supportive comments. However, when I got around to looking at the post weeks later, I realized she only had three comments, the first being my comment saying that I would get back to her, although I never did. I was so caught up in writing this book about my parenting mistakes that I didn't take the time to reaffirm to this young mom that she was not alone. I still feel bad that I never got around to responding. Most moms I know are in multiple mom groups on Facebook and sometimes cross-post. I hope she cross-posted as well and got enough responses to know that one embarrassing moment doesn't make her a bad mom.

HOUSE TRAINING

In 2003, we introduced our very first dog to our family of three: a black lab named Tonka who stole my heart. I'd never liked dogs or wanted one because they smell, but Joe kept talking about his childhood dogs. So one day, my mom, Sebastian, and I drove up to Dundee, Michigan, to get Joe a male black lab, which was the type of dog he always said he loved. It was so hard to choose a puppy—they were all so adorable. The one we really wanted was a skinny, chocolate female lab. She followed Sebastian around the yard, but she was $150 more than I had with me and Joe really wanted a male black lab. So I handed over $500 for our pureblood black lab and left with a cute, fat black puppy to surprise Joe.

House training Tonka was hard because Joe was literally never home. He was always at the office. So that left me to care for, train, and figure out what to do with this furry four-legged creature. Sebastian helped a lot and enjoyed taking on the daily tasks of training and caring for Tonka. He went so far as to help house-train Tonka.

One day after taking the puppy outside, he came in and asked, "Can I pee outside and show Tonka how to do it?"

I stared at him for a moment, thinking. Then I recalled reading in a puppy training book that if a puppy sees an older dog pee outside, the puppy will imitate the behavior and learn faster. Monkey see, monkey do, right? Maybe this would work.

"Uh, I guess so. Just make sure the neighbors aren't out."

"Yay!" he shouted as he ran outside with Tonka chasing, tail wagging.

This went on for a few days, until one day Sebastian came in while I was vacuuming the living room and announced, "Mommy, I just taught Tonka to poop outside."

"Great," I said. It took a minute for me to process what he'd just said. "Wait, what?"

"I pooped outside to teach Tonka how to do it. He watched me, then sniffed it. So now he knows how to poop outside!"

"No way...you really pooped outside?" I asked, not really believing what I was hearing. "Show me."

I followed Sebastian through the house and out the back mud room door to our fenced backyard. We had five-foot chain link fencing. He pointed to the ground near the door.

"See?" He was so very proud of what he'd done.

What I haven't mentioned so far is that, on this particular pleasant summer day, my neighbors were having a cookout. The grill was fired up, and people were outside with paper plates piled high with corn on the cob, fruit salad, baked beans, and hot dogs—and here was my three-year-old defecating in the grass just twenty feet away and in plain sight.

As I stood staring at his poop, I noticed a few neighbors looking at me. I was mortified. I wondered if they had noticed, or if they had just overlooked it as a little boy playing with his puppy in the yard. I wasn't sure, but the probability of at least one person seeing him was pretty high. I quickly ushered him into the house, away from the festivities next door.

In his mind, pooping was really no different than peeing, so if I said it was okay to pee in the yard, why wouldn't it be okay to poop as well? The neighbors never did mention anything to me, but I'm sure someone saw it.

CHAPTER 15

Germs!

WHAT GOES IN MUST COME OUT: THE VOMIT EDITION

Throughout my years of parenting, I have come to realize that I am not the greatest nurse to sick children. I have a very short fuse and don't want to hear the constant whining about something I cannot fix, especially when they refuse to do the things that will help them get better. If you have experienced this before, you know exactly what I mean. When my children were babies and toddlers, I'd hold them, stay up all night with them, rock them, soothe them, and coax them into drinking small sips of coconut water, bone broth, juice, or anything at all that would get fluid into them.

I recall when my youngest woke up from a nap very late one afternoon and vomited sage green, partially digested guacamole all over me and the kitchen floor. She was about eighteen months old. The look of panic in her eyes will be forever etched into my memory; the poor little girl had no idea what was happening. Let's face it, vomiting is one of the worst physical things you can endure during a common illness. When your body completely takes over, violently forcing liquid and solids up your esophagus in the wrong direction, it can literally lift your body from the floor.

This isn't to mention the traumatizing pain of dry heaving. When they were little, I would just lay a towel across my chest and hold them, keeping a vomit bucket and a new stack of towels nearby. I would let them throw up right on me and just switch out towels. When they were little, it was easier to deal with the sleepless nights, the crying, and the vomit-soaked towels because I knew they were terrified and helpless.

My best friend told me she doesn't mind sick children during a phone conversation when she had a sick child home from school. She said that she enjoyed the clinginess of her children when they're sick. She said that soon they will be all grown up and not want to snuggle with her all day on the couch. Never do her kids need her more than when they're sick.

I guess I just don't have that gene. I think of her sometimes when my kids ask me to lie with them when they are not feeling so great—we all have our strengths, and I recognize that dealing with sick children is not one of mine.

MY INITIATION INTO THE VOMITED-ON CLUB

When Sebastian was two years old and being extra clingy, he asked me to sleep with him. I was still a new mom, only twenty-five years old, and not nearly as wise as I am now. I later discovered that extra clinginess is a telltale sign of an impending illness.

Adults act like this too. When my husband is sick, he wants hugs and wants me to sit with him. I'm the same way when I'm feeling under the weather. Maybe this is a biological thing, to seek out others when you're feeling ill so they can help you not die when you're too ill to move.

There I was, sleeping next to my two-year-old in his full-sized bed when I was suddenly awakened by the heaving, gurgling sounds of vomit being spewed forth from my sweet boy directly into my long hair. The sour, acidic smell of vomit is unmistakable, but that night it also had a strong nutty odor.

When I got up to turn the light on, I realized that my long hair, which falls past my mid-back, was heavy and covered in vomit. As grossed out as I was, I grabbed my hair, shook out what I could, and threw it up in a messy bun to get the stench away from my nose while I cleaned up. I quickly changed my son's clothing and sheets, then wiped his sweet, flushed face with a soapy and damp rag. I looked at the pile of vomit on the sheets and saw bits of peanut. It was then that I remembered he had been snacking on peanuts after refusing to eat his dinner. This was not unusual for him—he was an exceptionally picky eater.

Joe had now made his way upstairs from sleeping on the couch. He was always quick to help with the clean-up from vomiting children. He collected the laundry and took it downstairs to start the rinse cycle on the washer while I sat with Sebastian, my hair still wet with vomit and partially digested peanuts. I rubbed his back and lulled him back to sleep.

I was finally able to sneak away and jump in the shower. My hair was partly dry by then, crusty and stuck together. I lathered up with copious amounts of fruity shampoo, not only to clean the vomit treatment currently in my hair, but also to cover up the noxious odor and prevent myself from vomiting right there in the shower. Talk about a "real" mom-life spa treatment As I scrubbed, I felt chunks of peanuts falling from my hair and gathering at the bottom of the tub. Oh no...I was going to have to pick up all those slimy peanuts that were once in my child's digestive tract but were now about to plug the drain.

Peanuts, why did I feed him peanuts?

I dried off, dressed, checked on Sebastian (soundly sleeping), and then headed down to the washer to check on the sheets Joe had thrown in. The cycle was done, so I started pulling the sheets from the washer only to discover there were peanut pieces still all over the sheets, just like my hair.

Gross!

Of course they didn't wash out—they were too big to fit through the washer holes. I would need to scoop them out and rewash the sheets.

I pulled each item out, shaking it onto the basement's concrete floor, scooped the peanut pieces from the washer, then placed the sheets back in to rewash them. I then grabbed a broom from the closet and swept up the floor.

Finished, I headed back up the stairs to the bedrooms to check on Sebastian. He wasn't too hot, but possibly had a low-grade fever. I was torn: should I lay next to him and end up with vomit in my hair again, or leave him to sleep on his own?

I decided to lay in his room so if he got sick again I would hear him, but far enough away that vomit wouldn't end up in my hair again. Just as I was falling asleep, I heard retching. I grabbed a bucket and ran over to him, but he was too little to know how to vomit into a bucket, bowl, or toilet. Again, he threw up all over the fresh sheets and floor.

This went on throughout the night. By 2 a.m., I didn't think there was much left in his little body. I fell asleep in my bed with Joe, thinking the worst was over. Sebastian fell asleep on the futon couch in his room.

At 5 a.m., I got up and checked on Sebastian. The smell hit me before I entered the room. It was a pungent cocktail of vomit and diarrhea. My precious little boy was sound asleep but covered in vomit and diarrhea.

I knew I had to wake him, but the smell was so strong that I had to fight the urge to vomit myself. I was crying inside and feeling like the biggest mom failure there ever was. He'd gotten sick all over himself, and I wasn't there to help him, rub his back, or even clean him up. He was lying in pure filth.

I got Joe, and we stared at him for a few minutes, trying to decide what to do. Finally, we felt it was best to wake him, strip his clothes, and move him to a clean area.

As I peeled the clothes from his weak body, I realized they were stuck to him. His skin was red and irritated by the acidic expulsions from his body.

How did I not notice that he was sick again…how did I sleep through it?

We put him in the tub to soak off the crusty vomit and diarrhea, then looked at the futon mattress. It was soaked and had no waterproof protection. A new mattress was only a couple hundred dollars, so we made the executive decision that keeping a stomach virus–soaked mattress was a bad idea. We dragged that mattress down the hallway and threw it over the second floor balcony onto the frozen grass below.

That's exactly where it sat after a winter rain soaked it the next day: frozen and too heavy to move. We were unable to move it until the spring came—gross, I know!

Sixteen years later, my husband and I still laugh at what our neighbors must have thought of us on that cold winter night when we threw a mattress over the balcony, then left it there all winter long.

WE DON'T CARRY "CHEAP" BOWLS

Recently, eight-year-old Tyler was at the mall with me because Alexis, age eleven at the time, had a Girl Scout meeting in a conference room on the upper floor of our mall. Tyler kept saying that his stomach hurt. I bought Jamba Juice smoothies for everyone, but Tyler didn't touch his. That's when I realized that something must really be wrong. I reached over and put a palm on his head to check his temperature. Yup, he was hot. Still complaining that his belly ached, I decided we needed to leave. We trudged up the stairs to get Alexis and tell her that we were leaving early.

I interrupted the meeting to say we needed to leave because of a sick child and handed Alexis a razzmatazz smoothie as we headed out the door. It was a rather long walk from the side of the mall we were on back to the van. The whole time we were walking through the mall toward the exit, Tyler was stopping every few minutes and dry heaving. I knew he was a ticking time bomb; I just didn't know when it was going to happen.

Will we make it to the van? Will it happen in the van? I hope not. That'll send everyone into a vomiting frenzy.

I saw a garbage can just ahead. "There's a garbage can...do you need to use it?"

He shook his head back and forth to say no.

"Okay, I need to run into Williams Sonoma and pick up the Instant Pot I just bought. They are holding it there so I don't have to lug it through the mall. I'll be fast, I just need to grab it."

I left three children standing outside the store in our indoor mall with Alexis. I quickly approached the counter and asked, "Do you have any cheap bowls I could buy?"

The saleslady looked appalled.

"We do *not* have any *cheap* bowls here," she sniffed with clear distaste. "We sell only high-quality items. We have a few less expensive bowls."

"Okay, how much?" I asked hurriedly.

She smoothed out her cream pencil skirt with her well-manicured hands and sauntered over to a blue bowl with her nose turned up in the air, as if she was better than me. She flipped it over slowly and said, "This one is only $39.99."

"I just need a bowl or bowl-like item to collect the vomit from my child who is currently standing outside your store dry heaving. I just don't want vomit all over my van on the way home!"

"Oh dear," she remarked, covering her hand over her mouth as her silver bangles softly chimed and slid to her wrist.

She walked very slowly back to the counter and held up a paper bag.

Is she serious?

I stared at her, dumbfounded. A paper bag! Had she never experienced the substance of vomit?

"Um, are you serious?" I said. "How is a paper bag going to help? You seriously have no plastic bags anywhere in your store?"

"We have garbage bags, but they're very thin." She started to line the paper bag with a thin plastic garbage bag just as my children barged loudly into the store to find me.

"Tyler is throwing up all over the front of the store!"

The saleslady shoved the bag to me and ran to the front of the store, grabbing the crappy $39.99 blue melamine bowl on the way.

Oh, now she wants to get me a bowl!

The saleslady saw Tyler's vomit all over the front carpet of the store and, with an exasperated sigh, turned and walked back inside. With a wave of her hand, she announced over her shoulder in disgust that she would call someone to deal with the mess! I secretly wished that I had dragged my heaving son into the store with me and had him vomit all over everything! Maybe she would have acted faster.

I rubbed Tyler's back and told him it was okay as the tears in his eyes told me how embarrassed he was to have lost the contents of his stomach all over the floor of the mall.

My other children were gagging and making a bigger scene, as children tend to do when something gross happens. I yelled at them to stop and reminded them how much this would suck if it was them. They quickly quieted down, content to make silent, gross faces to one another.

A small, very young security guard with blond hair in a pony-tail showed up and asked if we needed anything, and if Tyler was going to be okay.

"No, he's just sick. We couldn't make it out of the mall fast enough. I'm very sorry for this mess. Can you get me some paper towels so I can clean this up?"

"No need for that," she said. "There's a cleaning team on the way, and they'll take care of it."

She dug through her black first aid fanny pack and found a peppermint candy. "Would this help?" she said, holding it out and offering it to us.

"No, thank you," I said as politely as possible. I didn't want to go into detail on how adding red dye and high fructose corn syrup would be a bad idea. "Do I need to stay until someone shows up to clean this? I wouldn't want anyone to step or slip on this."

"No, you can go, that's why I'm here. I can make sure no one walks near this area. The cleaning people should be here any moment."

We walked outside into the dark, crisp winter air, which felt nice right then. There's something about cold Ohio winter nights that I loved. The sky seems clearer, the moon brighter, and the air fresher.

I drove home with the windows partly open, taking a few deep breaths as I thought about the sleepless night ahead, my hair in a bun and bleach water in my trusty spray bottle on standby.

Tyler had gotten some vomit on his coat, so despite the cold winter air we kept the windows open to ventilate the van. I blasted the heat to help warm the van, but it really didn't work.

Joe was overseas for work, leaving me alone to deal with the possibility of five vomiting children. The thing with big families is that sickness spreads like wildfire and most often hits everyone. Sometimes this happens quickly, with all seven of us racing for the toilet or bucket at the same time, and sometimes it happens slowly.

Just when I think that only one child will be sick, the next child gets sick. This can go on for weeks. However, on this particular evening we were blessed to only have that one vomiting incident. Tyler slept the rest of the night and had a fever for forty-eight hours. The rest of us were spared. This was a very rare occurrence, but the universe was looking out for us that day.

Some of the hardest parenting moments are when kids are sick. It's hard on your heart and hard on you physically. Even the house takes a huge hit—who has the time and energy to pick up the house when the people who dwell in it are sick?

HOW DID YOU MISS THE BOWL?

In 2019, my nine-year-old was complaining of a bellyache, so he was sitting in the bathroom. If you sat in the middle of the room you could literally reach the sink, the tub, and the toilet—not to mention he also had a vomit bowl in front of him.

Eleven-year-old Xander was in the shower in our small bathroom when I heard him yell, "Mom, Mom, Mooooooooooooooooooo ooooooooooooooom! Tyler is throwing up."

I was on the opposite side of our ranch house when I heard this. I slowly approached down the long hallway, only to find my son on his knees leaning over the mostly empty bowl directly in front of him.

Instead of in the bowl, vomit was sprayed across the bathroom floor, on the small turquoise rug in front of the sink, all over his pants, shirt, watch, and on the side of the small bucket containing items from his sister's fish tank, which she had neglected to put away after scrubbing them.

I stood there for a moment, staring at my child in bewilderment, confused as to how very little vomit had made it into the bowl, the sink, the shower, or the toilet. Xander was in the shower, so not throwing up in there was a kind thing to do—that would really suck if you were in the shower gettin' your scrubbin' bubbles on when a head pops in and showers your feet in vomit!

"How on earth did you manage to miss the bowl?" I asked in a very irritated tone.

"I don't know," he said. Did I really expect a logical answer? Cleaning up vomit is a disgusting, messy job, where you need to fight back your own urge to vomit the entire time. It's like cleaning up egg yolk from the floor: slimy, drippy, and full of mucus. Blech! I wasn't thrilled about the fact that my nine-year-old, who has had plenty of practice hitting the bowl, had thrown up all over the floor.

This is where I fail as a parent: I kept repeating loudly and with more irritation in my voice, "How on earth did you miss the bowl? Geez, you got it all over the rug too! Go stand over by the toilet as I clean this mess up." I made exaggerated movements as I scooped up vomit with paper towels and sprayed bleach water all over the floor. I knew my son felt badly about getting sick and I knew I was acting like an asshole, but like I stated earlier: I suck as a mom when my kids are sick!

I realized how nasty I was acting, so I tried to tone it down. I always apologize to my children for my poor behavior after the fact, and they usually respond with, "That's okay, Mom." But it's not okay. I think I've gotten better over the years, but I still suck at parenting sick children.

TRIED-AND-TRUE TRICKS OF THE TRADE

I have learned a few things over the last nineteen years when it comes to dealing with stomach viruses. First and foremost, they suck. They are yucky and contagious and the worst sickness to infect your house. Especially in a house with lots of people, it's inevitable that a stomach virus will run its course through everyone, sometimes twice!

Here are a few tricks I've learned along the way:

1. Keep at least enough buckets or containers for every person in your household, because at some point everyone will be sick at the same time. Extra buckets/bowls are also great to have on hand so you can quickly give a new bowl to a child while you whisk away and wash the one containing vomit.

2. Have designated vomit bowls. Nobody wants to eat pasta out of a bowl that contained vomit the previous week. Even if it's sanitized, that's just gross! I use clear plastic salad bowls from Bed Bath & Beyond. They're about 9.5 inches across and have a 4-inch depth. Having a shallow bowl works well when a child is lying down. A very important feature is a flat bottom—no one wants a bowl of vomit that can tip easily.

3. Keep waterproof tablecloths around, the bigger the better. Get the ones with the flannel backing so they stay in place and don't slide. You can find 90" x 108" rectangular tablecloths on clearance at many stores at the end of every season. I buy the smaller ones to lay out on the floor when the kids are painting or doing a messy project. I also lay these on the floors or couches to protect them from the noxious, smelly liquids that can be expelled from a sick child. I sometimes layer a sheet or towels over the tablecloth to add a bit more comfort, but I make sure my kids know

to stay on them. I have scrubbed tomato-based vomit up so many times from our carpet that I needed to find another way. These waterproof tablecloths have been a time-saver. If only I would have thought of this in my early parenting years. It took five kids before I realized this trick—you're welcome!

4. Keep bleach on hand. I usually keep a very natural home, using mostly vinegar and a few essential oils to clean. However, a stomach virus is just the thing that I pull out the bleach for. I have a bleach-only spray bottle that I use to spray and wipe down surfaces in the bathroom almost hourly when someone is sick (yes, this is probably overkill). I also use it to clean out sinks and vomit buckets. As for laundry, that gets a good dousing of bleach, as well as any underclothes, towels, blankets, and anything else vomit could be on, or that would have been touched by an infected person. I treat a stomach virus as if the plague has hit our house.

5. Out of respect for all humans, I follow the guidelines that the CDC (Center for Disease Control and Prevention) recommends and don't let any infected child leave the house for at least forty-eight hours after the last episode of vomiting or diarrhea. I also warn any friends or family that a stomach virus has hit our house, and leave it up to their discretion if they choose to be near us. An infected person can remain contagious for up to two weeks!

6. I always keep gentle, stomach-friendly foods on hand to ease solids back into my kids after they've been sick. Getting sick always happens at the most inconvenient of times, and sometimes I'm acting as a solo parent, so a trip to the grocery store is not always an ideal situation. I always stock applesauce, coconut water, Great

Lakes gelatin to make squares, bone broth, eggs, and ginger or mint tea to ease belly discomfort. You can also use a grocery delivery service in an emergency.

CHAPTER 16

Take My Breath Away

The scariest and the most heart-wrenching moments of parenting are when your child is hurt or you fear for their life. Never will we love anyone on this planet more than we love our own children. Without a thought we would take away their pain if we could, but we cannot. None of us have a magic wand or a manual in our birthing kit. We have to endure the really hard stuff.

JUST BREATHE

I have ridden in an ambulance twice during my forty-two years of life, and neither time was as exciting as it looks through the eyes of a small child when they are zooming down the road, lights and sirens blaring, shouting, "Look! Look!"

My second child Alexis was only fourteen days old when I rode in an ambulance for the second time. We were temporarily living with my mother-in-law, as the company Joe was building was sucking the life out of us and every dime we owned. I had maxed my student loans to invest in his company, and we had taken out multiple bank loans and borrowed $30,000 from my father. We couldn't afford to stay at our first house on Drummond Road anymore. I had to file for bankruptcy.

The universe
HAS A STRANGE WAY
OF GIVING YOU JUST
WHAT YOU NEED,
WHEN YOU NEED IT
MOST,

even if you don't see it right away.

I loved it there; it was my favorite house. It was outfitted with beautiful honey hardwood flooring throughout, a gorgeous bay window to let in the afternoon light, and a fenced yard for the children to safely play. This was also the street I had grown up on, just thirteen houses down from where my mom and dad lived, and it was within walking distance to a quaint neighborhood park. This was the house I saw us being a *real* family in.

The backyard was so full of memories: ice cream dripping down our chins in the summer after a long day playing in the hose, or the Fourth of July that I sat outside with Sebastian swatting at mosquitos with our new puppy while fireworks lit up the sky. We raked leaves and jumped in the piles. We carved pumpkins and set them aglow on our porch on Halloween night. We built snowmen, made snow forts, and had snowball fights every winter. We planted flowers in the spring and watched the daffodils peek up through the snow every year.

This was how my life was supposed to be—this was the house that all my dreams would come true in. *This* was my happily ever after.

The universe has a strange way of giving you just what you need, when you need it most, even if you don't see it right away. I was five months pregnant with Alexis when we packed up our house.

I fought back the tears as I pulled away, leaving my favorite house in the rearview mirror while Sebastian cheered in the backseat that were headed to "Moose's" house. This was the name he gave to Joe's mom, because her last name was Moses. We called her Mema Moses, but one day Sebastian decided this was too much to say and he mashed the two words together to create "Moose." From then on, my mom was just plain Mema and Joe's mom was Moose.

Moving in with my mother-in-law was not what I had planned. I had always felt like she never liked me, but she opened her small house to us and did everything she could to make us feel comfortable. It was hard learning to live with her, not because she wasn't welcoming, but because I felt like I was giving up my dream.

Joe was always at work, so it was just the three of us most days: Sebastian, my mother-in-law, and me with a growing belly full of life.

A few months after we settled in, and just after Alexis was born, I headed outside with the kids. Alexis was fourteen days old and had only been home from the hospital for ten days. After she was born, she needed to stay in the NICU for a few extra days because her lungs were slightly underdeveloped, and she was jaundiced.

The sun was shining brightly on this beautiful spring day, so we headed outside to help with Alexis' bilirubin. I sat in a white plastic lawn chair in the backyard watching six-year-old Sebastian play with his basketball. Alexis was wearing just a diaper, and I was holding her against the exposed skin of my own belly and breast as I nursed her in the sunshine.

Joe surprised us and came home early from work at 6 p.m.. He sat outside with us for a bit before we headed inside.

Later that evening, Sebastian was asleep tucked in bed and I had just finished nursing Alexis. I laid a blanket on the floor in front of the TV and placed Alexis on top to change her diaper. My mother-in-law was sitting just two feet away from me watching a movie on the Hallmark channel.

I looked up at the TV for a second after I was done changing Alexis and putting her in a sleeper. When I looked back down, I saw her eyes roll back in her head. Her lids fluttered, her head turned slightly to the left, white foam formed at her mouth, and her body became very stiff. "Donna! Something is wrong!" I yelled.

She jumped up and flipped Alexis over her arm with her head down, hitting her back to clear her airway. I stood there frozen, watching my mother-in-law. I had faith she could fix my baby. She was a registered nurse on the cardiac floor at our local hospital, so I felt she had more skills than I did and knew just what to do. After just a few seconds, Alexis started turning blue. "She's not breathing," Donna said, her voice cracking. "Call 911!"

I ran for the phone and shouted for Joe. "Alexis isn't breathing!" I said, crying and fumbling with the phone. I was shaking badly, thinking Alexis was dying right here, right now.

Joe snatched the phone from me to do what I seemed unable to do. I looked at my mother-in-law; she had Alexis flat on her back and was slowly forcing air into her little body by placing her mouth over Alexis's nose and mouth. I thought the worst, but there was nothing I could do at that point. I raced to our bedroom, ripped off my pajamas, and threw on some clothes. I grabbed my purse and a diaper bag, pausing to glance at my six-year-old, who was sound asleep.

If I'm going to lose any child, at least it's not Sebastian.

I hated myself the minute that thought popped into my head. How could I think such a thing? I loved my children so much, how could I value one life more than the other? The answer was as simple as time. I had only known Alexis for fourteen days outside of the womb. I had only fourteen days of memories with her.

Did I love them the same? Yes, of course, but I had six years with Sebastian to make so many memories. What if I never got those memories with Alexis?

What if fourteen days is all I will ever have?

In the living room, Joe was on the phone with the 911 operator and my mother-in-law was holding Alexis upright. She said to me with a shaking voice, "She's breathing, but not regularly…it's just not right, her breathing is off."

I was afraid to hold my baby, afraid that a change in position would stop her breathing. So I rubbed her head and talked sweetly to her until the paramedics arrived. Upon arrival they checked her vitals, asking lots of questions while they unloaded all sorts of medical contraptions onto the floor.

"She appears to be stable now, but you should have her checked out right away. You can either drive her to the hospital yourself right now or we can take her."

"Take her," I blurted. "I want her there right away. Can I go with her?"

"Yes, your husband can follow and meet us there."

I grabbed Alexis' things and put her in her car seat. They secured the seat to a gurney in the back of the ambulance while I rode on the bench next to her, watching intently for any sign of distress. I recall the emergency workers talking to me, but I cannot recall what was said. All I could do was stare at my tiny baby and wonder if fourteen days was all I was going to get with her.

We arrived at the hospital in record time, and they got right to work in a flurry of activity, exchanging information with a full room of doctors, nurses, and phlebotomists. They undressed her and started the process of drawing blood and getting an IV started, but her veins were so tiny that the ER nurses could not get the needle in. Three nurses tried multiple times with no luck while Alexis screamed. I was a wreck seeing her in distress like that.

A young red-haired nurse looked at me and said, "At least we know she's breathing well with a scream like that." I think she was trying to make me feel better. Clearly, she was too young and inexperienced to understand that those words are no help. A mother would understand. I managed a weak smile, knowing she meant well, but my heart was shattering right there on the hospital floor.

Finally, they brought in a specialist from the pediatric intensive care unit. I studied her as she prepped to do what others before her had failed to do. I saw the needle that I hoped would make it into the vein of my little one—then I noticed that her panties were showing through her very see-through white scrubs.

Why on earth is she wearing panties with red hearts? She must know they can be seen through her scrubs.

That was what I chose to focus on at that moment, the nurse in her see-through white scrubs and her red heart panties. I find this slightly humorous—I guess it was easier to focus on the silliness of her clothing rather than on the seriousness of what was happening.

Alexis was calm by now; I was nursing my sweet little baby and she was wrapped up in her pale pink cashmere blanket. The red-heart panty nurse approached us and said, "You can keep holding her. I just need an arm." She gently pulled her left arm loose and carefully slid the needle into a vein on the first try. This heaven-sent nurse managed to do what three nurses before her couldn't. She got the blood work finished and an IV started in a matter of seconds. I was impressed.

"Wow! Thank you so much...that was amazing. These other nurses have been trying for over thirty minutes, poking my baby over and over."

"Well, it's my job to poke little babies," she said, smiling warmly. "I work on small babies all day long. Their veins are trickier and very delicate, but once you get the hang of it, it's rather simple. Plus, I hate to see little babies cry, so I was a quicker learner."

"Thank you so much," I said as she walked out of the room, and I giggled as I watched her walk down the hallway with small, bright red hearts plastered across her rear end!

Alexis continued to have short seizures in the ER, but she was breathing okay. They decided to admit her to see if they could figure out what was causing these episodes. While they were getting a room upstairs in the children's wing secured for her, I stepped out and left her with Joe while I headed to the bathroom. When the door was shut and locked, I began to cry.

What if I lose my baby? How could I have had those thoughts about losing her over my oldest? What kind of mom thinks that way? What did I do wrong? Why is this happening? Am I being punished?

I only allowed myself a few minutes for my private pity party before pulling myself together and heading back to the room.

When it was time to move Alexis to her permanent room, she was asleep on my chest. They wanted me to wake her and place her on the gurney. I protested and asked if I could carry her, but they said no. We finally compromised by having me sit on the gurney while I held her so she could stay asleep, undisturbed. I strolled with her in style, imagining I was atop a chariot instead of this sad and scary reality.

We passed through multiple bright hallways with animal murals painted on the walls and play areas before entering the magenta door that led to our room. This section of the hospital was vastly different from the drab beiges and whites of the ER.

We stayed in the hospital for five days. I held her the entire time. I was afraid if I walked away or set her down, she would seize again and stop breathing. I put her down only to use the bathroom, and that was only when I felt as if I was going to burst and the nurse was in the room doing vitals.

I was exhausted. I held her sitting up in an orange vinyl chair, afraid that I would doze off and drop her. I was grateful for the hospital staff, who brought me bland cafeteria food and juice as a courtesy because I was exclusively breastfeeding.

Joe stopped by for a few quick visits to check on Alexis, but he never stayed long. He thought I was neurotic for holding Alexis nonstop. He had to get back to work so that someday we could afford a house of our own again.

My mother-in-law was a huge help during our stay in the hospital. She worked at the same hospital on a different floor, and she would stop by after her shift to hold Alexis so I could stretch my legs or get in a quick nap.

Knowing that my daughter was in the capable arms of her loving grandma and a registered nurse, I decided to walk up and down the halls to stretch my legs and release a cramp in my hip. I rounded the hall past a lavender painted door when another mom emerged from the room.

She must be stretching her legs too.

Her dark hair looked straggly and unwashed like mine, and her clothing was rumpled as she walked in a daze, lost in thought. She looked up to meet my eyes. They were streaked with red and framed by dark circles.

I must have looked the same, although I had not managed to look in a mirror for days. We *felt* each other's pain. This deeply moving moment, shared in silence, spoke to me in a way that words couldn't. We shared pain, hope, and sadness all in one gaze. A soul-penetrating pain that can only be caused by a mother's unconditional love for her frail, sick child. We both managed to muster a weak smile as a symbol of hope and encouragement, then walked our separate ways.

I think of that mom from time to time and wonder if everything turned out okay for her. I have never experienced the loss of a child, but my heart breaks for those who have.

Sometimes we just bury

THE REALLY HARD
STUFF BECAUSE WE
FEAR BEING

vulnerable.

After countless tests, including a spinal tap that I wasn't allowed in the room for, the doctors were still baffled. They couldn't figure out what was wrong. She continued to have very small seizures and issues with breathing.

Minutes, hours, and days ticked by, and I continued to hold her. I held her for fear of losing her, but I also held her out of fear that these might have been my last moments with her. It's strange how quickly life turns in a direction you could have never foreseen.

During one morning shift change, I was sitting in my orange chair with pillows propped around me and my sweet Alexis soundly sleeping on my chest. I was lost in thought when a nurse barged in abruptly, flipping on the main lights and flooding the room in a bright fluorescent glow. I saw her blurred figure walk toward us, my tired eyes adjusting slowly.

"I need to check her vitals. Place her on the bed."

"Um...no!" I was astounded by her rudeness. "Can you just check her from here? She's sleeping."

"I guess," she scoffed. "But that's just not the way we do things."

"We have been here for three days and all the nurses before have done checks while I held her."

There was an awkward silence while she got to work, being unexpectedly careful not to wake her. It was surprising to see how gentle she was with Alexis after her abrupt entrance. "All set. Things look good. Any questions or concerns?"

"No."

She wrapped her stethoscope around her neck, grabbed her things off the bed, and shoved them into the pocket of her teal Alice in Wonderland scrubs. I never much cared for Alice in Wonderland, which was just how I felt about this nurse. She turned around, pausing with her hand on the doorknob, to say, "You know, you don't have to hold her all the time. The night nurse said you never set her down or left at all. You can leave her in the crib, she'll be fine. It's our job to take care of her here, not yours. We can do it more efficiently without you in the way."

Really? Wow, like I needed permission to set her down. How could a pediatric nurse be that rude and uncompassionate? She should work on another floor, like with patients in a coma. Or better yet, in the morgue.

We never did get any solid medical answers. They sent us home with an apnea monitor that Alexis was supposed to wear to track her breathing and heart rate. It would sound an alarm if there was an inconsistent pattern.

While I was writing this chapter, I happened to talk with Joe about my thoughts I had about losing Alexis over Sebastian. He said he'd never heard that before and had no idea I'd had those thoughts, which is false because I did share it with him at the time. He then went on to lecture me, saying, "How on earth could you have those thoughts?"

Seriously?

I had just explained to him how I had those thoughts and how bad I felt about it. I still beat myself up over it.

These thoughts are hard to put into words and even harder to share with others. I wanted to cut the part of this essay when I had the thought about losing one child over another. I kept it because if it helps just one mama, it was worth it. Alexis, when you read this, please know that I love you more than words can say. I also want all you mamas reading this right now to know that none of us are perfect. Sometimes we just bury the really hard stuff because we fear being vulnerable.

DON'T RUN WITH SCISSORS

My kids loved to play with scissors when they were young. They would watch me use this magical tool to transform something into a new shape. Looking through a child's eyes, I guess this strange metal tool does seem quite magical.

We tell children not to run with scissors, but I don't know anyone who has actually been injured by being impaled with scissors. I'm sure someone, somewhere has, which is why the rule became famous.

Over the years, my children have had many run-ins with scissors. I once found my eighteen-month-old cutting his own amber teething necklace from his neck. Another time, I found one of my children, age three, in the bathroom cutting his clothes off his body before his bath.

A favorite playtime activity of mine is using plastic Play-Doh scissors to cut apart long rolls of Play-Doh. Hey, ya gotta find amusement sometimes with kids' toys in order to stay sane. My children never want me to sit and watch them; they always want me to play along. There is something very satisfying to me about cutting rolls of Play-Doh into pieces.

But none of these run-ins with scissors were as terrifying as the day that the walls of my house looked as if a gruesome murder had just occurred.

2016

I was sitting at my desk, idly going over our schoolwork for the next week and plugging in tasks and topics for the next month. My desk sits at the end of a long hallway at the farthest end of the house. Behind me, I heard Tyler (age seven at the time) shuffling slowly toward me with a slight whimper. As he came nearer, I could hear fear in his feeble voice. He was throwing a red string at the wall as he stumbled forward.

Why was he throwing a red string?

He came within five feet of me, and before any words were shared, I was sprayed with a very thin stream of blood. It happened very fast, and then stopped and started again.

Shit! This is an arterial bleed.

Blood was shooting out with the rhythm of his racing heart. I leaped forward and grabbed his hand, squeezing hard and holding it above his head. Blood trickled through our entangled fingers and dripped down his forearm, creating a small pool on the floor.

"Mom," he said, looking for reassurance. I could tell he was terrified. His cheeks were damp with tears, and his eyes fear-stricken and dilated.

"Everything is okay," I said. "What happened? Did you cut your finger off?"

I was too afraid to let go and release the pressure on his cut.

"What were you doing?" I said.

"I don't know!"

I was confused—how did he not know what he was doing?

I was still holding tight to his hand and applying more pressure than maybe was necessary.

What do I do next?

My mind raced as I tried to locate the memories buried deep in my cerebellum. I guided him into a sitting position in case he passed out.

I looked around the room, trying to figure out what to grab or do next, knowing that I was not going to release his hand no matter what. Only a trickle of blood was seeping through now. Holding his hand high and applying pressure was doing the trick.

I took a deep breath. Sebastian was sitting nearby at his desk with headphones on, not knowing what was going on behind him. He had recently taken a course at the university and was a Red Cross-certified first responder.

"Hey!" I yelled loudly to get his attention. As soon as he saw the pool of blood on the floor and the blood all over the walls, he went into a bit of a panic, walking in circles and trying to wrap his brain around what to do.

"Call 911!" I shouted.

After he gave the 911 dispatcher all the information needed to find our house, he handed the phone to me. They asked more detailed questions, but I couldn't answer most of them because I had no idea what had really happened.

"Is his finger still there?"

"I don't know."

"Can you see bone?"

"I don't know."

"Can you look?"

"Absolutely not," I said. "I will not let go and stop applying pressure until the paramedics are here. I have no idea of the damage, but when I'm holding tight the blood flow is minimal."

"Okay, ma'am, they're on their way. Just minutes now and you should see them."

Sebastian waited by the door to show the paramedics in and guide them to us. They could've really just followed the path of blood.

These glorious men paraded through the door with my son leading them. It seemed like lights were shining down on them from above…okay, the only light shining down on them was from the 1970s fixtures in our outdated house. They were here to help, to save my son. It was then that my heart finally started slowing to a normal pace. I still think of them as amazing men with jobs that save lives. They expertly carried in all sorts of bags and gear, prepared for most situations.

The lead paramedic headed right over and sat next to us, talking to my son in a very gentle and calm voice, asking questions about what had happened. I let go of his hand and was shocked to realize that there was no more blood shooting from his body. The blood had coagulated, and I was feeling like a complete idiot for calling 911.

Feeling the need to defend my decision to call them, I said, "I swear this looked bad. Blood was shooting from his hand a good five feet. Look at the front of me, look at my walls!"

"I see that," the paramedic calmly stated while looking directly into my eyes. "You did the right thing calling us. He definitely cut an artery, and your fast action caused it to stop bleeding so quickly."

"I thought if you hit an artery, you were as good as dead. That's why people slice open their wrists to kill themselves."

"In some cases yes, but he seems to have just nicked the artery, so his body was able to fix the issue with the help of your fast action. If you hadn't acted as quickly as you did, we may have walked into a completely different situation."

The paramedics wrapped his finger and did not bat an eye when I handed them our tube of Colloidol silver instead of the Neosporin they offered to apply to his wound. The paramedic was familiar with Colloidol silver and supported its use—not that I needed his support. Usually when I try to treat anything holistically, I get eye rolls and displeasure from most mainstream medical professionals.

That day will be forever burned into my mind. How absolutely terrifying it was to see the blood shoot from my child's body!

I asked my son later what he was doing that got him cut. You want to know what his response was? He was cutting out the cute lemon character from the box of our lemon twist all-natural Earthpaste. Every time I see a tube of this toothpaste, whether on my bathroom counter or on the shelves in our favorite health food store, I'm reminded of that day.

STATS AND STUFF

According to the New York State health department, choking is the fourth-leading cause of unintentional death in children under the age of five, and in most cases, the children are choking on food. As shocking as it seems, at least one child dies every five days from choking. FIVE DAYS! Every year, twelve thousand children in the US seek medical treatment for choking-related injuries.

Would you know what to do if you saw this happening?

Cardiac arrest in infants is not as common as choking, but it can happen—and the training for both occurs in the same class. Take the class, mamas. I didn't take the class, but thankfully someone else did and was there to do what I couldn't.

I cannot stress the importance of CPR classes enough. After Alexis's problems, I have stayed mostly up to date with trainings, sometimes lapsing a year or two between certifications. I have taken classes in person, taught by paramedics, been trained by the Red Cross, and taken online courses through the Red Cross and other sources. I feel they are all good—just go get certified. It can seriously save a life. Most courses will teach infant, child, and adult CPR because the process is slightly different with each.

As part of these classes you will also learn how to treat a choking infant. I once had to flip one of my children over and do back blows and chest thrusts when a small strawberry became lodged in my child's airway.

If my mother-in-law hadn't acted so quickly, my daughter could have ended up with severe brain damage or worse. If we hadn't moved in with my mother-in-law and lost the house that I *thought* was my dream house, Alexis may not be here today. The universe really does work in strange ways. I am a firm believer that everything in life happens for a reason, and I believe that moving in with my mother-in-law saved my daughter's life. Blessings in life are sometimes hidden within disappointment—you gotta look hard for that silver lining.

Of all the CPR classes I have taken, none were as informative as one taught at the library by the Rossford fire department. They shared with us that if you're doing chest compressions on an adult correctly, you will feel and hear their chest crack.

What? Really? Oh yes, it's true!

I recently connected with Ashley, a local firefighter mom. During our conversation, she stated that on occasion she has run into CPR instructors who didn't even know about hearing and feeling the chest crack during compressions.

Ashley went on to say that she has experienced this firsthand. "It's a sigh of relief when you hear it the first time, because you're like, oh my gosh, I'm actually doing it correctly."

No one ever told me this in ANY class I have ever taken. I feel like this is something they should tell everyone, because if I'd ever had to do CPR and I heard and felt that, I may have stopped immediately, thinking that I killed the person I was trying to save. I have never had to give CPR to anyone, but I feel confident that I could.

Blessings

IN LIFE ARE SOMETIMES
HIDDEN WITHIN
DISAPPOINTMENT—

*you gotta look
hard for that silver
lining.*

CHAPTER 17

Social Media Sinkhole

Every day, I feel like I am failing at this parenting job. I know I'm not, but I'm so hard on myself. The explosion of social media has only made it much worse. Constantly being bombarded by beautiful images and magical moments...it takes a lot out of me.

Sometimes I have to take a deep breath, step back, and center myself, knowing that maybe these moms had a good day or moment but they're not as perfect as the picture or post portrays.

They, too, have bad days and moments of doubt in their lives. Just like I stated in the chapter "Zen Music and Bacon," my breakfast spread did *look* picture-perfect, and I posted that picture because I was proud of my accomplishment. But the moment was not nearly picture perfect.

I UNFOLLOWED YOU ON FACEBOOK, THEN YOU UNFRIENDED ME IN REAL LIFE

In the mid-2000s, when I was in my late twenties and early thirties, social media was just beginning to bloom. MySpace was the first social media site I'd heard of, but only my friends who still lived a single, childless, nightclub life were on it, so I had no interest.

I was too busy juggling dirty diapers, laundry, and home-schooling to sit on the computer any longer than necessary. But then fellow moms started asking me to join them on Facebook. I resisted at first, but in 2012 I created my first Facebook account and joined the 1 billion current users.

Facebook added a whole new element of gathering friends, and now there are pictures...lots of them. A picture is worth a thousand words, but whose words? And what words? A picture can invoke emotions that have nothing to do with the actual image.

Humans are naturally curious creatures, so we scroll through people's photos and look through their posts to catch up. We get so caught up in how amazing someone else's life looks that we start to compare our worth to their perfect moments. But no one posts their worst moments.

Social media took us all on a whirlwind. It was amazing how easy it was to share and connect with people you already knew and make new connections with people you didn't know. I lived through this change and have seen how this has affected friend-ships. Many of my friends have gone through periods of "social media detoxing." This is when they temporarily disable their accounts to get away from the drama.

A few years back, I was in a bad place. I was depressed and had a scare with a decent-size tumor (it was benign). My cancer scare made me reevaluate what I was really getting from social media.

On July 4, 2016, I wrote in my old blog that I was leaving social media. I stated, "Social media is something I need to step back from." Here is what I wrote:

I hope my friends take the time to read this...

I have decided that, for me, social media is something I need to step back from. It's necessary to connect with cus-tomers for our farm and to stay connected to some home-school pages that I run, so I am not disabling my account, but I will be limiting my time and unfollowing all friends.

I was using Facebook to enjoy social interaction with adults. I'm home all day with five kids and a husband who works long hours and is out of town monthly. So for me, it was a way to maintain sanity and have adult conversations.

Something changed over the years on Facebook—or maybe I changed. I started to find myself itching to check my news feed more and more often (like an addict looking for a quick fix of happy). Yet I soon found myself not getting any "happy" from it. I started to find myself wishing for more and more of what I didn't have.

The people I'm friends with on Facebook post highlights of their seemingly perfect lives: their awesome husbands, the new stuff they just bought, their great vacations, their very perfect lives. I would sit there with chicken poop on my boots in my dirty and outdated 1970s house feeling inadequate.

I kept checking Facebook...spending WAY more time than I ever imagined. I was looking more and more for my "happy," only to find less of it. I was ignoring the giggles and joy of the children playing outside and catching dragonflies by the pond. Facebook was a nasty drug addiction, and it was getting bad!

So I unfollowed all my friends. Yup, every single person. So if I don't like or comment on something you post, it's because I didn't see anything on my news feed. If I want an update on a friend, I need to go to their Facebook page to see it, or I'll just give them a call. There's a button on Facebook that hides all the posts made by your friends, and they don't know you did it. I wanted my friends to know this so that when I wasn't commenting on or liking their posts, they wouldn't take it personally.

This did not go over as well as I expected—I lost some friends over it. One friend in particular stated that if I was her "*real* friend"

Friends will come
and friends will go,
AND IF YOU ARE
CHANGING AND
GROWING AS A PERSON
IT MAKES SENSE THAT
your social circle
will change and
grow as well.

and important to her, I would want to know what was going on in her life all the time. This is the same friend I routinely called a few times a month to have an actual conversation with. In fact, it was during a phone conversation that she shared this information. I was very hurt since we had been friends for seven years, but what was I going to do? She made her choice, just like I made mine.

Some friends stay in our lives for a lifetime and others for just a short season. Not every person you meet is going to be that friend who is sitting in the bingo hall with you at age seventy-two or holding your hand on your deathbed. Friends will come and friends will go, and if you are changing and growing as a person it makes sense that your social circle will change and grow as well. I guess if she was that affected by my unfollowing her, maybe she was not the close friend I thought she was.

We all have our journeys in life. Sometimes we are walking the same path, and sometimes we choose different paths. It's rather sad when these changes happen, but we need to live our lives for ourselves and not for other people. I'm the most important person in my life. I come first. If I don't put myself first, everyone around me is not getting the best version of me, and that's not fair for anyone. I implore you to do the same.

My ex-friend and I run into each other from time to time, and we exchange pleasantries, even an awkward hug once. This took my daughter and me both by surprise. It was a little confusing that she cut me out of her life, but then initiated a hug. Still, I hugged her back, knowing that she must have needed that connection. I was glad to see she was doing well and living her life in a way that suited her best. It's not the quantity of friends in your life, it's the quality.

You are the handful of people you choose to be around. Think about that. Do your closest friends bring out the best in you? Do you leave them feeling happy? Inspired? Or are you leaving them with negative thoughts? A bad attitude? Or do you maybe even leave and then complain about them?

It's hard to make the cut in life, and it can be even harder to realize that you were the one cut from someone else's life. When this happens, take it as a blessing. Your friend simply realized first that your journeys do not align, and you need to move forward separately.

To this day, her and I continue not being friends. I wish her well, and I am truly sorry if my unfollowing her on Facebook hurt her, but I needed to do what was best for me and my family.

During my time away from social media, I spent more and more time outside with my kids and really being present. The craziest thing happened during these frequent trips out to the parks and other places. I ran into many friends, and we would ask questions about life, homeschooling, parenting, and just spend time catching up. I sometimes commented about how I had to back off social media, and guess what? They did too!

After my six-month social media detox was over, I started following friends again slowly, but I found myself happier and didn't need to keep up on all the people I was friends with on Facebook.

I worked hard on establishing relationships that meant a lot to me with face-to-face get-togethers, such as coffee dates, or nights out for drinks and appetizers. I started a local book club and realized that getting out was vital to my sanity. I couldn't just use social media as my main form of social interaction.

Over the last few years, I have noticed more and more of my friends posting about leaving Facebook, detoxing from social media, or texting me to let me know how to reach them. I have seen many friends disable their account for a while, then pop back on months later stating they just couldn't take it anymore. Type "Facebook Detox" into a search engine and you'll find pages upon pages of reasons to step back from social media and methods to do it.

My favorites are the famous YouTube streamers talking about why they had to stop, how it affected them, and why or why not they went back. I'm not the only one feeling the need to step away from social media!

When I look back, I realize that when my kids were younger and no one was old enough to stay home alone or watch other children, Facebook was my only option. Going back before Facebook existed, I used Yahoo groups and mothering message boards to socialize with other moms. This was vital to my survival, as I really needed a mom tribe. These boards were focused on supporting moms, and it was just words, no pictures.

Don't let social media be the last thing you see at night before you go to bed. Turn your phone off and put it on the other side of the room. Spend a few minutes reflecting on your day, not what you did *not* get done but what you *did* get done.

When I lay in bed at night, I wonder what I could've done differently that day, if I could've been a better parent. Then I try to focus on the best things that happened that day. Think of this as a mental gratitude journal.

Shut your eyes and breathe deeply. Think about the things that went well that day and cement those images in your mind before you fall asleep. Maybe even get a journal and write it down. Think of moments that made you smile, moments that made you laugh, and moments that made your heart sing.

Watch out, though, because negative thoughts love to creep in during this time. I mentally fling those thoughts far away. I imagine I am holding a slingshot, and as I pull back hard and let go, they fly far away and I think, "Not today, negative thoughts. Not today!"

Then I go back and imagine myself in a field of wildflowers, high on a mountain, with the sun shining and fluffy white clouds floating past in the bright blue sky. I recall the best moment of each day. In doing this, the last images in my head as I close my eyes each night are the happy, positive ones of my life, not the perfect pictures on social media that sometimes leave me longing for more of what I don't have instead of focusing on what I do have.

Once you make this a habit, life completely transforms. You start looking for the good in everything and focusing on being productive. And once you are focused on being productive and positive, you start actually being productive and positive. You are your thoughts, so be very careful of the thoughts you let dwell in your brain.

CHAPTER 18

Mama, You Can Do Hard Things

I hope this book helps you know that you are enough and that we are all trying to do the best we can, even when our paths are very different. There's no right or wrong way to raise children. We are all so very different from one another, but I know that we all share the mutual goal of raising happy, healthy children.

This book was hard to write. As I wrote each section, I relived every moment. My heart raced as I told the story of Bailey being forgotten in the car; I cried as I wrote about losing Xander at the zoo; my heart sank and my hands shook as recalled the story of Alexis turning blue; and I laughed when I wrote about putting together a makeshift diaper at the grocery store.

What kept me writing was my mom and dad. Although they are not physically here, I felt as if they were right there, next to me. I felt a hand on my shoulder as I hunted and pecked for each letter, giving me the support I needed to keep going.

Every day that I sat down to write, I walked around the world a better person, a happier person, a more sympathetic person. I have learned to forgive others, but most importantly I learned to forgive myself.

We've all had bad days, and even the best parents have moments when they lose their shit. I recall seeing a mom screaming at her kid in a public bathroom. I thought, "Gosh, what an awful mom. Why would you act that way? I never would." Oh, but I have!

I don't like to admit that I have screamed at my children, but some days are just too much. Although I judged that mom, fast forward two years and she's now my friend. She's a really good mom who is kind and caring, but on that day she was having a really bad day. We've all had them.

Through writing, my eyes were opened. This book literally changed me and created a better version of myself. Funny that the book I wrote to help others was the book that made me a better person.

Most of all, I wrote this book for you and for all the other mothers out there struggling to be that picture-perfect mom.

SOME BACKGROUND ON JOE

Joe is the loving father of all five of our children—he was featured in the background of many of these stories. I tried to exclude him as much as I could, because this book was not about him, but he does appear from time to time when important to the story. So I thought a little background may be helpful.

We do not have the typical relationship of most married couples. We were friends who ended up together after he moved to North Carolina with me in 1998 after a hard breakup. I was escaping to North Carolina as well due to heartbreak. We found comfort together going through the same thing, but other than that we are extreme opposites.

Joe had a horrible relationship with his father, never speaking to him after Joe turned eighteen. He never wanted children for fear he would turn out like his dad.

I, on the other hand, had always wanted children, but was told I could not have them due to a variety of medical conditions.

When I found out I was pregnant with our first child, I was over the moon excited. Joe was not thrilled—he did not want children.

The first year was hard. I suffered from postpartum depression while I lived in a house with a man who loved his son but resented me. Joe spent as little time as possible around me so he could continue to be there for his son. He worked long hours, providing me the opportunity to be a stay-at-home mom, which I am forever thankful for. He spent any free time playing games on his computer or at a game room he and his friends rented in the office building we now own.

I was a solo parent.

Over time, our relationship drew closer and he stopped resenting me. In 2004, he started his own business to provide our family more income and a better life while I worked part time at a nightclub and attended the University of Toledo.

In 2005, when things were going good, Joe asked if I would be open to adding multiple children to our family. I didn't know if we would be able to conceive again, but I was so excited by his change of heart. Three months later, I was pregnant with Alexis. Turns out I have NO issues getting pregnant...Joe and I are both extremely fertile.

I had to quit my job due to pregnancy complications, which left us with a huge income drop. Joe had to work harder to support our family and keep his newly started business afloat. This put a lot of strain on our relationship; we had no idea how we were going to pay our bills. I pulled out the maximum amount of money I could from my student loans to help us through this, but eventually I had to file for bankruptcy and we had to move in with my mother-in-law for a year.

Joe went back to never being home; he worked eighteen-hour days, weekends, and holidays. We were in financial ruin, and he was desperately trying to pull us out of poverty. He didn't know how to deal with the overwhelming stress of it all, so he kept his distance from us. When he was home, he would unwind from the stress by playing games online and ignoring us.

Now it was my turn to resent him. I couldn't understand why he would offer to have another child but then ignore us when he came home. I was solo parenting again! It wasn't until this year that we talked it through, because I knew he would read this book.

He said the reason he stayed away so much and immersed himself in video games was to prevent himself from lashing out at us because of the high stress he was under. He thought by distancing himself that he was doing the right thing. He had no idea how much I was hurt by this because I had never shared my pain with him until recently.

As his company flourished, so did our family, with the birth of Xander in 2007 followed by Tyler in 2009. As his company expanded faster than our family, he continued putting in long hours with no weekends or holidays off. We bought a house close by the office, and despite his long hours he made it a priority to come home each day to share a meal as a family, then back to work he would go.

Since the birth of our first child, Joe managed to pull us out of poverty. He got us off welfare and made it possible for us to live a more relaxed, comfortable life, no longer worrying if our lights would get turned off. This took a lot of sacrifice, including some blood, sweat, and tears. Joe is hardworking, perseverant, and unstoppable when he puts his mind to it. A great role model for our children.

In 2012, things started to settle into place with Joe's company, opening up more time and causing Joe less stress. A few years later, we added our last child, Bailey, and bought a large, outdated, ugly farmhouse on fifteen acres.

Our relationship has never been easy. In fact, it's been downright hard. We are literally opposites, right down to my favorite color being white while he favors black. Life with him is hard, challenging, never easy, and sometimes I stop to wonder if that's what keeps us together, because easy is boring.

We are alike in some ways. We are both very stubborn and hard-headed, which is one of the worst things we could have in common, but we work through it, sometimes with the help of a therapist.

We do not have a picture-perfect marriage, but there is beauty in imperfection. What we do have is the drive to put in the time and work that it takes to make us stronger. We are most certainly a work in progress, even after twenty-two years, and I imagine we will be until the day we die. That's the key to a strong marriage: knowing that it's always going to take work.

LETTERS TO MY CHILDREN

I realize that if you read this, you may be full of many emotions. All are valid. Your father and I love you more than words can say. It's true I have made many mistakes, and sometimes you have felt the blow of one or more of them. I'm sorry for that; I would never intentionally hurt you. What I want you to know more than anything is that perfection is an unattainable goal. We are all flawed, and that's okay; no one was meant to be perfect. Don't be afraid to fail, because failing is an opportunity to learn. Carve your own path in this world and know that I will always love and support you. The road will be hard, but I will stand beside you. Anything is achievable if you set your mind to it!

Dear Sebastian,

Although you were an unplanned surprise, you were deeply loved from the moment you were conceived. It's true your father was against your birth, but it was only because he deeply feared he would ruin and damage you like his father did to him. No wound cuts deeper than that of the person you love most hurting you. Your father loves you.

You will always be my miracle baby, because I thought I couldn't have children and then you came along. I hoped you would be a 6 lb. little girl, but the universe had other plans and you were a beautiful chubby 9 lb. 11 oz. boy who stole my heart.

Unfortunately, you were our rough draft, our firstborn child, and we made the most mistakes with you. I'm sorry for this, and I'm sorry I broke your magic sword from the wizard shop.

It's hard to believe that you are twenty years old, a man, off on your own now and living the life you want. I am so proud of all you have accomplished. Dream big, my son. No, scratch that, dream bigger than big, because you can do hard things. And to steal your own words from your 2019 news interview, "Anyone can do anything if you want it bad enough."

Love,

Mom

Dear Alexis,

When I was pregnant with Sebastian, I wanted a girl. So when I found out I was expecting you, a beautiful girl, I was thrilled to pieces and hurried off to the store to buy all the pink things. I clearly remember a soft pink elephant with lavender ears that played lullabies. I would press it to my belly so you could hear the song, and long after you were born, I pulled the string on that pink elephant and played that lullaby for you as I nursed you to sleep next to me.

You terrified me in utero when you constantly had hiccups and I wondered what was going on. Then you scared me even more when I was told of your heart murmur after you were born with underdeveloped lungs and whisked off to the NICU, when you stopped breathing and turned blue at fourteen days old, when you continued having seizures, when we realized your tonsils were obstructing your airway and causing you detrimental breathing issues, and when your tonsils were taken out. You've had a rough start, but no other child was held more and more constantly watched. I was so scared I would lose you, but you are a fighter with a strong will. You are a woman of indomitable spirit.

However, you are an incredibly sensitive child. This may be your greatest strength, but also your greatest weakness. You feel deeper than the average person. You stand up for others when you see injustice. But you take on so much feeling and pain from others that I see how it weighs so heavy on your heart. If I could take away all the heavy that rests on you, I would. It breaks me to see you sad.

You are an amazing person and I thank my lucky stars to have a daughter like you, even when you're being sassy, because it lets me know that you will do alright in the world. You will stand up to others, you will not be a sheep, and you will achieve anything you put your mind to.

Love,

Mother Dear

Dear Xander,

You are my Dr. Jekyll/Mr. Hyde, maybe not as extreme as the 1931 movie portrays, but it explains your personality. You have two extraordinarily strong sides: a sweet, kind, docile one, and a highly active one, quick to anger. I love them both because they are you, and you are amazing. As you have grown, you have learned to control these mood swings, but I see how hard it can be for you. Even in utero and as a small baby you would act this way. All day long, you would be so calm in my belly, only moving gently, then out of nowhere you would jab me in the ribs. There were times this sudden cobra strike would cause me to jump, shout in pain, and even drop me to my knees. Then I would rub my belly and think that I couldn't wait to meet you.

As the middle child with light brown hair, you make sure you are never missed or forgotten. Not only do you look so much different from your siblings, your personality is different too! It's good to be different, always remember that. You keep your sweet side hidden, but I know it's there. You have a fantastic imagination and can charm the wits out of anyone you meet. You are great with your hands, and you may soon kick my butt in an arm wrestling match. You are so much smarter than you believe you are...I see it, I know it's there.

You are unstoppable and will conquer this world on your terms.

Love,

Mama

Dear Tyler,

You are my fourth child and my biggest baby of all, weighing in at a whopping 10 lbs., 6 oz. You were a chubby baby with big, beautiful eyes. Not only do you have eyes like an owl, you are quiet and wise like one too. You watch everything around you and silently observe, picking up skills by just watching. You are courageous and determined when you set your mind to something.

I was excited to discover that we share a love of the natural world. I love packing up hot tea and snacks early in the morning and heading out to birdwatch with you at our favorite spots. You always find the coolest nature surprises on our property, and I will forever cherish my vase of Blue Jay feathers.

Although you haven't quite figured out who you want to be yet, you are still young. I have faith you will find the path that is right for you while you sit and watch from high in the trees with your big beautiful eyes.

And thank you for catching that typo in chapter 16 late one night as you read over my shoulder, not yet wanting to go to bed.

Love,

Mom

Dear Bailey,

You are my last child, the baby of the family. We planned on giving you a sibling close to your age, but after I birthed you, I was told my baby days were over. I see how hard it must be as the youngest in a house full of people twice your size.

You have a strong personality and you are a joy to be around. You are one spunky, spirited lass!

It will be a joy to watch you grow and flourish into a woman. I can't wait to see the mark you will leave on this world.

Love,

Mommy

All the Great Things I Have Mentioned in My Book

I mentioned a few books and products that you may want to check out. I am not sponsored by any of them. These are products I love, and I believe you will too.

For your convenience, I have also included a page on my website www.betsyharloff.com/bookresources for direct links. Please consider purchasing through those links. I do make a ridiculously small percentage off items purchased through Amazon, but every little bit helps. Thank you.

They are listed in the order they appear in my book.

The Omega Diet: The Lifesaving Nutritional Program Based on the Diet of the Island of Crete by Artemis P. Simopoulos and Jo Robinson
An oldie but a goodie. This book provides timeless health information repeated in most of the newer health books. Getting in the right type of Omega-rich foods can benefit you immensely.
https://amzn.to/3kPTCJp

mberry Miracle Fruit Tablets
Want to surprise your kids and make lemons turn sour?
These berries are a blast, you won't be disappointed.
https://amzn.to/307k6Oz

Super Taster PH strips
These are great fun to see which of you or your family members are super tasters. You can add in a whole genetic testing element, throwing in some learning, or just use the strips for fun. How many of your friends and family members do you think are super tasters?
https://amzn.to/3czvl95

Maddi's Fridge by Lois Brandt and Vin Vogel
Sweet story with a serious message about a young girl shocked to realize her friend's fridge was empty. She tries many humorous ways to bring her friend food without drawing attention to it.
https://amzn.to/35WziSh

101 Amazing Picture Books to Read to Your Child by the Toledo Library
This Picture Book Challenge was designed to provide children with a variety of books. Librarians chose 101 of their favorite picture books, from new titles to classics and everything in between. You can see this list online, I have provided a direct link on my website. You do not need to be a local library member to access this list.
These book choices brought up many great conversations that we would not have had otherwise. It also introduced us to authors and titles we may never have come across otherwise. *Maddi's Fridge* was one of those books.
Our library has been such a huge part of our lives, always providing great programs, resources, and activities for kids. I'm sure your library is the same. Don't miss the great

opportunities your local library could be offering you, I urge you to go today.
https://www.toledolibrary.org/

Laura Vanderkam's TED talk: How to gain control over your free time.

This twelve-minute talk changed my life and the way I look at whether I don't have enough time, or something is just not a priority. Definitely worth the watch. Go to www.betsyharloff.com/bookresources to find the direct link to her talk and my favorite book by her.
https://www.ted.com/talks/laura_vanderkam_how_to_gain_control_of_your_free_time

Diastasis Recti: The Whole-body Solution to Abdominal Weakness and Separation by Katy Bowman

If you have had a child, this is a must-read book for you. She helped me understand the mechanics of what my body went through and how to repair it.
https://amzn.to/3mWYjD2

MUTUSYSTEM

This program is worth every penny. I lost 20 pounds and rehabilitated muscle damage from carrying five children. I stand 100% behind this program.
https://mutusystem.com/

Fire Safety

For ideas, crafts, and downloadable checklists for kids and adults to keep your family safe. Head over to my website.
www.betsyharloff.com/bookresources

Exploring Nature With Children—Raising Little Shoots

A fantastic resource to get parents and kids outside exploring and learning about nature with hands-on activities.

We love this curriculum, her Pinterest account, and her website, which is filled with fantastic nature ideas. https://raisinglittleshoots.com/

The Power of Habit: Why We Do What We Do in Life and Business by Charles Duhigg, Mike Chamberlain, et al.
Great book on changing the patterns in your brain to break bad habits.
https://amzn.to/3mW0QgL

You can find direct links to all the products mentioned above on my website. If you purchase or use any of the above mentioned items, I would love to know what you think. Tag me on Instagram @betsyharloff or use the hashtag #notapictureperfectparent.

Acknowledgements

Writing a book about failure proved so much easier than writing these acknowledgement pages. I feel it's utterly impossible to put into words my appreciation for so many who have joined me on this journey.

Thank you to Sebastian, Alexis, Xander, Tyler, and Bailey, my children and my greatest teachers. You are my biggest supporters who encouraged me to write every day. Sometimes convincing me to write just so you could play Minecraft for hours, then convincing me to get Chick-fil-A for dinner so I didn't have to cook. I have grown and become a better person because of each one of you. I am inspired, challenged, and stronger every day because of all of you. Without you, I would have never known it was possible to love this much. You are my light, forever shining, even on my darkest days. I have failed you at times, but I hope I have done right by you more times than not. I'm forever learning how to navigate the world of motherhood with each new stage you reach. I love you each very much.

Thank you, Joe, my dear husband. You knew I was struggling with this section of my book and stated that I didn't need to thank you. How could I not thank the person who has given me the ultimate gift of becoming a mother? Without you, my biggest dream of becoming a mother would have never come true. You are my biggest supporter and believe in me more than I believe in myself.

Thank you, Kristin Wilhelmi, my best friend. You let me ramble for hours, offering constant support, always being my sounding board. The universe brought two Catholic schoolgirls together on their first day in the Toledo public school system. A friendship was born as we sat side by side in Mrs. Donahey's science class, and what a duo we have been ever since. We have lived an adventurous, sometimes dangerous life and it's a wonder we are still breathing. I can't imagine going through life without you. I hope our children find a friendship like ours. I know you and Joe both didn't want/need an acknowledgement, but I do my own thing: **"You can't tell me what to do!"**

Thank you to my Mom and Dad, who will never hold this book in their hands. Losing a parent is devastating, losing two is indescribable. It's a very strange feeling indeed to no longer have any living parents. I was lost when my dad died suddenly of a heart attack alone in his apartment, ten years after my mom lost her life to cancer. I had just told him two months prior that I was writing this book. I stopped writing, devastated I would never be able to hand him my book. Six months later, I took my laptop graveside, laid out a blanket, and wrote most of the first draft next to him.

Thank you, Donna Moses, my mother-in-law. You brought Joe into this world and into my life. Joe and I have had our fair share of problems, but we love each other unconditionally. He is the yin to my yang; we complete each other. You are the most giving person I know, forever putting everyone else's needs before yours. You have opened your house and heart to me and are forever there for me whenever I need anything. You are an amazing grandma, whom your grandchildren adore more than words can say, and you saved Alexis's life with your swift action and medical knowledge. She is now a thriving fourteen-year-old because of you. Thank you for being you.

Thank you, Sherry Stanfa-Stanley, author of the book *Finding my Badass Self: A Year of Truths and Dares*. You took time from your busy life to sit with me at Rosies, offering wisdom and advice to the very naïve writer I was at the time. It was your valuable insight that sent me to the Michigan Writing Conference, connecting me with so many insightful people. I met my first aspiring writer friend there, Patricia Mcquire-Hughs. I hope to hold her book in my hand someday.

Thank you, Elaine Spencer. You were the first writing agent I met who believed in my book but felt my platform was not big enough for a publisher to take seriously. I cried in the gym when I opened your rejection email. I'm thankful you said no because my writing was crap then. It has come a long way since that day. Sometimes no is a gift we don't always see.

Thank you to Jon VanZile, my editor, and the team at Dragon Tree Books who helped bring this book into the world. You truly made me a better writer. Who would have thought that my daughter would meet the son of a published author and editor at Camp Storer during the exact time I was searching for one?

Thank you, Rebecca Ahern, owner of Axiom Lux. Your services and botanical infused products really helped a girl out when stress levels were at their peak. Writing this book was hard, but your products made it a bit easier. Keep shining your light, Becky.

Thank you to the writing community on Instagram—I have met some amazingly supportive friends there.

A big thank you to all those who beta read this book and offered valuable recommendations, most of which were implemented.

Lastly, I would like to give a shout-out to all the moms out there at whatever stage of motherhood you are in. This job is hard, confusing, and draining, but never will we love anyone more than our children, even when they won't stay in bed and we have to pause our show 3,000 times.

Children will remember
HOW HAPPY YOU WERE,
not how perfect you were.